The User's Guide to Being Human

The User's Guide to Being Human

The Art and Science of Self

SCOTT EDMUND MILLER

SelectBooks, Inc.
New York

Important Note

This "self-help" book is designed to support your own efforts in developing the extraordinary human capacities with which you were born. It does not provide medical, psychiatric, or financial advice; the tools and techniques presented here do not replace the counsel of a qualified financial advisor, nor do they replace the professional care of qualified physicians, therapists, counselors, nutritionists, or other licensed specialists.

The material in this book explores *general* human abilities and capacities. It does not describe the *specific* physiology, psychology, or life-experience of any one, individual reader. If you have health, emotional, or financial issues, be sure to consult a proper authority who can evaluate your unique situation and advise you accordingly.

Copyright © 2012 by Scott Edmund Miller

All rights reserved. Published in the United States of America. No part of this book may be reproduced or transmitted in any form or by any means, graphic, electronic, or mechanical, including photocopying, recording, taping or by any information storage or retrieval system, without the permission in writing from the publisher.

This edition published by SelectBooks, Inc.
For information address SelectBooks, Inc., New York, New York.

First Edition

ISBN 978-1-59079-212-4

Library of Congress Cataloging-in-Publication Data
Miller, Scott Edmund.
 The user's guide to being human : the art and science of self / Scott Edmund Miller. -- 1st ed.
  p. cm.
 Includes index.
 Summary: "The author examines eight human inner capacities by which people shape their lives. He outlines a step-by-step program to harness this great potential freely available within people to bring out the best in themselves and create the life they dream of leading"--Provided by publisher.
 ISBN 978-1-59079-212-4 (pbk. : alk. paper)
 1. Self-actualization (Psychology) 2. Self. 3. Self-realization. I. Title.
 BF637.S4M5486 2012
 158.1--dc22
                                  2011010550

Designed by Janice Benight

Manufactured in the United States of America
10 9 8 7 6 5 4 3 2 1

For you

CONTENTS

PREFACE

Everyone has inside himself a piece of good news! The good news is that you really don't know how great you can be, how much you can love, what you can accomplish, and what your potential is!

—ANNE FRANK, teenage author (1929–1945)

Life is an artistic process. Whether we are aware of it or not, we sculpt ourselves with every thought, every behavior, every action. We hold extraordinary creative power within ourselves, yet many of us tend to harness only a fraction of this power. As a result our art only partly achieves its great purpose, that of bringing out the potential magnificence in ourselves, our relationships, and our world.

Imagine a husband and wife, both made of clay. Imagine that one day they scrape together some extra clay and begin to work at it. It is soft and malleable in their hands and quickly takes on recognizable shapes. A little clay body forms, then little clay arms and legs, even a little clay penis and—presto, it's a little clay boy.

With great love and commitment, mom and dad mold in the boy their dreams of what he might become. Before long, little clay brothers, sisters, and friends come along. They too work at the boy, playing with him, challenging him, pushing and pulling at his form. Teachers appear along with aunts and uncles and neighbors and grandparents. All take turns working at the boy, sculpting in him that which they feel best suits him.

From time to time, when the clay boy has a moment to himself, he wonders about what he is becoming. He enjoys the moments of quiet, free from the constant poking and prodding at his being. He lies in the grass and watches the clouds roll by, fascinated by how mysteriously their forms shift as they cross the sky.

As the days and months pass, the boy finds himself subject to an increasing number of elements in the world around him—elements like peer pressure, grades, television, marketing campaigns, and scary questions like "What are you going to be when you grow up?" Weathered by these and other forces, the clay boy begins to harden.

One day he finds himself feeling rather fixed and inflexible. Fearing that his formation is nearly complete he looks to the clouds, asking, "Is this what I'm supposed to be?" The clouds drift by, shifting their forms, seemingly indifferent to his concerns.

Not long after the experience he falls in love with a young woman. They marry and soon create a little clay girl of their own. This new, soft little bundle of love fills his heart to the brim. Any worries about his own form are instantly put to rest. He silently promises to sculpt in his daughter all the things he wishes that someone might have sculpted in him.

Years pass, joyous years, during which the spontaneity and enthusiasm of youth begin to call upon him once again. He eventually begins to wonder:

> *What if I am like the clouds?*
> *What if I can change my form at any time?*
> *But how?*
> *How does one shape one's self?*

In a swell of inspiration he goes to the store and buys a bunch of self-help books, each of which offers some useful tips. He finds a therapist who, by exploring the elements that caused his hardening, helps him to recover some of his softness of form, his youthful flexibility. Then, at forty years of age, he finds himself at the start of a new life.

Sadly, he notices that his sixteen-year-old daughter is now harder than he. There in her form he sees so many qualities of his old self, qualities that he had molded in her. He tries to share his new tools with her. He tries to share his therapist with her, but his daughter turns him away in resentment about all her years at the hands of other sculptors, and for the unacknowledged pain that this creative manipulation has brought on. In an impassioned grab at self-expression and individuation the girl begins to acquire a series of unusual body piercings.

One night beneath the stars as he lies in the grass beside his wife, the clay man thinks to himself:

What if our child had held the tools of self-development
when she was soft and young?
What if she had learned to masterfully sculpt her own being?
What self might she have created?
And would that self include so many piercings?

We are all born with the tools of our own sculpting innately hardwired within us. Yet we are raised in a society that teaches us to be overly dependent upon peers, parents, teachers, politicians, counselors, medications, media, a host of commercial products, and other external factors. Many of us pass through the prime years of our development without ever really learning to use the intrinsic tools of personal development.

Whether you dance, draw, make music, shoot field goals, build houses, tune engines, or sit around all day watching television, you are an artist. Your single greatest work of art is your *self*. As with any art form, the more you understand and develop your talents, the more empowered and masterful you become as an artist. This is particularly important when engaging in the art of consciously shaping your own life.

The User's Guide to Being Human examines eight of our greatest inner capacities as artists, those underlying talents that drive our personal growth each day. Compiling thousands of years of human inquiry into the nature of learning and development, this work aims to help each of us understand and make use of the tools that are freely available within us.

Imagine a coming of age ceremony where a teenage girl—accomplished in using the tools of her ongoing personal development—takes over as head craftsman of her self, celebrating the end of a long apprenticeship, the end of childhood. Imagine a world where everyone consciously makes art of themselves each and every day by continually crafting themselves into greater quality works. Imagine families and communities of artists openly sharing their tools and techniques with one another.

What might that world look like?

Acknowledgments

One must find one's own voice, while acknowledging that, in the
oralist context, voice is never really exclusively one's own.
It is equally shared by others who have informed or inspired it.

—GRACE NONO, contemporary musician and culture bearer

Many thanks to those who supported the creation and publication of this book, including Steve Traum, Dr. Maria Schmeeckle, Julie Dubow, Richard Dickson, David Pollock, Sue Bryan, Danielle Zucker, Raymond Adelman, Kate Sage, Sally Rosloff, Cooper Zale, Heather Ashton, Kirk Ward and Tracy David. Additional thanks to the many teachers, students, colleagues, friends, family members, and world citizens I have had the privilege of knowing—each of whom has in some way helped to shape this work.

Special thanks to: Kenzi Sugihara, Nancy Sugihara, Kenichi Sugihara, and SelectBooks; Dr. Jean Houston; Bill Gladstone, founder of Waterside Productions; Janice Benight, who designed the book's interior; Pamela Rice, who designed the book's cover; my parents Norm and Jill, and my extraordinary family.

The following thinkers have laid important groundwork for certain key concepts developed in this book: with much appreciation, I acknowledge Albert Einstein for his famous formula $E=mc^2$, and Carlos Castaneda for his studies of *personal power* developed upon in Chapter 1; Jean Piaget for his theory of *Constructivism*, and Harvey Jackins for his insights on *emotion* developed upon in Chapter 2; Sigmund Freud for his insights on *projection* developed upon in Chapter 3; Dr. John Kappas for his studies on the mind and hypnosis developed upon in Chapter 4; Carlos Castaneda for his studies on the *nature of reality*, and Sigmund Freud for his work on the *ego* developed upon in Chapter 6.

HOW TO USE THIS BOOK

The mind, once expanded to the dimensions of larger ideas,
never returns to its original size.

—OLIVER WENDELL HOLMES, U.S. Supreme Court Justice (1841–1935)

The purpose of this book is to offer a crash course on some of the most important aspects of your humanness—those inner capacities that you probably had little time to discover while you were busy getting a formal education, busy going to work, or busy struggling to survive. Each chapter explores an essential human capacity that is freely available within you—a tool for creating the unique life that you might dream of leading.

I've titled the book *The User's Guide to Being Human* because it is intended to serve as a practical handbook. It provides guidance for developing your innate capacities while *using* them in the context of your actual, everyday life.

As the preface suggests, we are all artists; we craft ourselves, our relationships, and our world with every thought and action. Similarly, we are all scientists; we naturally use scientific method each day in the automatic process of learning and growing:

- We observe things.
- We ask questions about the things we observe.
- We develop hypotheses—possible answers to our questions.
- We experiment, testing to see if our answers are correct.
- We ponder the results, and then start the process all over again.

In 30 years as an educator, human development theorist, and school developer I have found that many of us grow up believing that only certain among us are artists, that certain others are scientists, and that the rest are neither. This is an erroneous belief that disconnects many of us from our true nature. I have subtitled this guide *The Art and Science of Self* because it is designed to stimulate and support a balanced use of these two, innate aspects of our humanness.

Philosopher and politician Confucius long ago said, "I hear and I forget; I see and I remember; I do and I understand." This guide is not meant to simply offer food for thought, but to provide you with numerous opportunities to awaken and reveal the immense potential available within you. *To know something* in-and-of itself is of little value. To *apply what you know* is to give your knowledge actual, concrete value.

The exercises at the end of each chapter enable you to actively develop the various capacities explored in that particular chapter. Consider four options on how to proceed:

1. Basic Study

Simply read through the chapters and exercises and let the information float about in your mind. If you find that a certain concept doesn't seem to make sense along the way, don't worry about it. By the time you finish the book you will see the big picture. The little pieces will make more sense within the greater context.

2. Intermediate Study

Take time to actually engage in the exercises chapter by chapter. In doing this, you will nourish both the art and science of self. Much like pursuing a personal Ph.D., this experience will deepen your understanding of the material. You will develop greater effectiveness in using your innate capacities and will empower yourself to more consciously shape your own life. See page 184 for *User's Guide* Support Materials.

3. Collaborative Study

The appendix at the end of the book provides information on how to form a "Reflection Group," which significantly enhances the "Intermediate Study" experience as you share it with colleagues, friends, and/or family members.

4. Advanced Study

Visit usersguidetobeinghuman.com where additional information, coursework and support is provided.

Keep in mind that the concepts presented throughout these pages are not offered as any form of ultimate truth, but rather as useful ways of looking at the human experience. Their purpose is to be practical—to offer specific tools that empower you to consciously influence how your life unfolds.

Introduction:
Befriending Your Inner Thinker

What we think, we become.

—BUDDHA, teacher and founder of Buddhism (563–483 BCE)

Thinkers are often viewed as heady intellectuals, those strange people who live to grind numbers and write inaccessibly technical papers. We might imagine them tucked away in universities and corporate think-tanks pondering endless details about terribly complicated matters. At the same time, we might also question the extent to which their work holds any real-world value, especially to us common-folk and our everyday lives.

Whether we recognize it or not, *thinking* is one of our most fundamental human activities, arguably the primary tool of personal development. It requires no diploma, no degree or certification. It happens within us each and every day, awake and asleep, in love and alone, employed and unemployed, sober and inebriated.

Every living person from the infant to the aged continuously develops ideas on a host of important matters. *Who am I? Why am I here? Will I ever figure out how to use this darn remote control? What are my limits? What possibilities exist for me? Why do things happen the way they do? Are relationships always this complicated, or is there just something wrong with me?*

With every thought we have, we address these and other questions. We explore the issues and experiences that affect us from day to day. Our thoughts form the foundation of our actions and behaviors, profoundly shaping our lives. Some of the thinking that we develop guides us toward success and joy. Other thinking sets us up for failure and heartache.

I met my own inner thinker on January 27, 1991. I was hanging out with a bunch of buddies at a local Superbowl party, engrossed in one of the great football games of all time. Ottis Anderson had just run one yard for a touchdown, giving the Giants a 17 to 12 lead over the Buffalo Bills—this after a triumphant 14 play, 75 yard drive up the field.

Relieved from the tension and excitement of the game by a commercial break, I scurried off to the kitchen in search of munchies, where I stumbled upon a most unusual sight. There on the floor, all alone in the middle of the kitchen, was a baby girl. She was seated cross-legged, gazing intently at a line in the linoleum floor. She seemed transfixed, scrutinizing the line as if it somehow held a secret to the universe.

I was a young teacher at the time, and as such had also become a student of human nature. Fascinated by the child's fascination, I sat down on the floor beside her—if just for a moment—to see what she was up to.

She stared ponderously at the line, and then quite unexpectedly she reached out to pick it up. Much to her surprise, the line would not pick up. She tried again, and again, and after a series of failed attempts turned helplessly to me. A terrible squealing sound began to emanate from somewhere deep inside her. She burst into tears.

Rather unfamiliar with babies, I swallowed awkwardly and stared at her, hoping that her mommy (or any available mommy) heard her crying and was quickly on the way.

"So-phie," called a man from the living room in a singsongy voice. "You're all right honey," he said warmly. He waved at baby Sophie and promptly returned his attention to the television advertisements.

Though daddy had already turned away, she glanced in the direction of his voice, stared blankly for a moment, then gazed down at the floor once again to continue her examination.

She gave another long, careful look at that line in the linoleum and glanced around at some of the other lines across the floor. Noticing her foot there among them, she grabbed at it instead. A bright smile lit up her face as her pudgy little fingers tightened around her pudgy little toes. She tugged gleefully at her foot, nearly tumbling over.

Infected by her enthusiasm, a big, dumb smile spread across my cheeks. It was a wonderful moment, the two of us smiling mirthfully at one another. We were both very happy about something, though I wasn't quite sure what it was.

Sophie bobbled to the left, swayed to the right, yet managed to reclaim her balance. She peered down at the line in the linoleum once more. She stared at it for a long moment and then glanced back at her foot. Then back to the line. Then back at her foot. It was like watching a scientist engaged in experimental observation—albeit a very small scientist, wearing only a diaper.

Once again Sophie reached for the line, and once again she was unable to pick it up. But this time, rather than erupting in a fit of tears, she grabbed her foot with one hand and reached for the line with the other. Upon discovering that the line was still ungraspable, a charming little baby-giggle bubbled out of her.

I could hear that the game had started up again. Yet at that very instant, it occurred to me that I had come upon baby Sophie in a most portentous moment. Much like Copernicus discovering that the earth was not in fact at the center of the universe, baby Sophie, right there in the middle of the kitchen on Superbowl Sunday, was discovering that not everything in the world that can be seen can also be held. To my amazement, she was making this rather sophisticated discovery all by herself.

I was anxious to get back to the game, yet I couldn't help but watch as Sophie's inner thinker exuberantly tested her discovery again and again across various lines in the floor, giggling more exuberantly each time she got the same result.

"This line is a two dimensional thing," I began to explain, temporarily forgetting that she was a baby. "It's just a pigment printed on the floor. Your foot, however, is a three dimensional thing." She watched me as I spoke, focusing her attention on the movement of my lips. I began to feel somewhat foolish and chuckled to myself.

Sophie smiled. "Gak!" she proclaimed. She grabbed her foot and moved it in my direction as if trying to show me something.

In the moments that followed, I found myself thinking quite a bit about our encounter. I realized that by grabbing her foot and raising it toward me, Sophie had tried to share her thinking with me, just as I had tried to share my thinking with her. Each was a work in progress, more sophisticated than it once had been, yet less sophisticated than it might become.

I returned to the game in time to join a testosterone-driven ruckus of argument over a failed play. My buddies and I spiritedly assaulted each other with speculations about why the game was going the way it was and what might happen next. Our inner thinkers were boisterously active, awakened by the sheer volume of masculine bravado. I began to notice that we weren't just arguing about football, but about strategies of effective action, teamwork, and partnership. That's when it hit me.

By milling about through various daily experiences and interacting with other people and things, our inner thinkers continually ponder everything under the sun, including the nature of self, relationships, competition, cooperation, values, spirituality, the laws of the universe, and so on. These thoughts lay the groundwork for every detail of how we live our lives, for our effectiveness and folly alike.

Highly successful people tend to develop *highly useful thinking*; less successful people tend to anchor themselves in *less useful thinking*. To witness this principle in action, you might interview a prison inmate—preferably a repeat-offender—who, like the rest of us, can't help but share his or her thinking on life. You will find within that person's thinking the roadmap to incarceration, regardless of the individual's intelligence level or genius.

Observing baby Sophie as the thinker within her worked to better understand the laws that governed her universe, I began to wonder how it was that my own inner thinker could have gone unnoticed for twenty-five years. Did it have something to do with growing up in a society where the "authorities" on just about every topic were always people other than myself?

Schools often teach us that learning is a process of memorizing and recalling facts. We take tests and get grades, evaluating our success in absorbing the thinking of others, yet we often find ourselves with little opportunity to formally advance our own thinking.

This book is designed to collaborate with your inner thinker. While exploring various techniques in the art of personal development, you will uncover key thoughts that you have subconsciously developed over the years. You will have numerous opportunities to evaluate and advance your thinking, and to tailor this thinking to serve the highest hopes and dreams that you hold for your life.

We tend to get overly caught up in the "truth" of a thought or idea, making it rigid and inflexible, halting its development. The real value of any idea is not in its degree of truth, but rather in its degree of *usefulness*. It is not the word of God or any ultimate authority, but simply a mental tool used to increase one's understanding about the nature of things, allowing us to proceed with some degree of effectiveness in our everyday activities such as work, play, self-development, relating to others, leadership, parenting, and living life to the fullest. The best thinking, therefore, is the kind of thinking that is always evolving.

As you proceed through the following chapters, remember:

- We are all thinkers.

- The thoughts that we hold greatly influence every aspect of our lives.

- The value of a thought is in its usefulness, not its rigid claim to truth.

- We update our thinking through daily ponderings, conversations, studies, and experiences, thereby updating our understandings of the laws that govern the universe.

- Some thinking developed in childhood remains rigid and unchanging, causing childlike behaviors to carry over into our adult lives. By re-evaluating this thinking and advancing it, we develop new behaviors that better suit the adult lives that we most wish to lead. We set ourselves up for greater success in everything we do.

For many of us, our inner thinkers were ridiculed, thrashed, and thwarted during childhood. We learned to glaze over any time we started to hear something intellectual or complex sounding, and found ourselves suddenly apprehensive, feeling inadequate or uninterested. We said things like, "I don't get it," or "This is boring."

This was the result of improper schooling, not of deficiencies in intelligence.

Like Sophie, you developed thinking on the nature of complicated subjects such as dimensionality when you were just a baby. Regardless of your life-conditions, work or educational status, you are a powerful thinker. As such, *persistence* is your simple and elegant key to progress. As theoretical physicist Albert Einstein once said, "It's not that I'm so smart; it's just that I stay with problems longer."

This book will help you to advance your thinking in a number of practical areas, and if necessary, will nourish your confidence in the process of doing so. If you don't give up, the thinker within you is bound to become more powerful and successful with time. The value of this pursuit is eloquently revealed in the words of essayist and poet Henry David Thoreau who said, "Thought is the sculptor who can create the person you want to be."

A Note to Readers

Stories are used throughout this book to illustrate various concepts in action. Most of the stories are based on actual occurrences, but the names and identifying features of characters have been changed to protect the privacy of individuals portrayed. Some poetic license has been taken in order to clarify key points.

Part I
Empowerment

———————

Energy is the substance of life. It nourishes our bodies, minds and hearts. It drives our actions, thoughts and feelings. If we wish to lead powerful lives, we must learn to consciously finesse the multitude of energies that are available to us each day.

This part examines the nature of energy and personal power. It presents four arts that promote success, health, and vitality.

Essential Questions

Take a few moments to ponder the following questions. Allow yourself to come up with at least three answers to each question as a means of self-discovery. This is an important step in developing the "science of self." Keep a written record of your answers in a log or journal.

- What most drains me of my energy?

- What aspects of my life feel the most invigorating and empowering?

- What might it take to more fully awaken and command my own sense of personal power?

CHAPTER 1

The Art of Empowerment

In the depth of winter I finally learned that there was in me an invincible summer.

—ALBERT CAMUS, author and philosopher (1913–1960)

Every once in a while, an individual comes along who seems to accomplish extraordinary things in life. He or she may be an athlete, an artist, a scientist, an entrepreneur, a dreamer, or highly successful in some way. Others often stand around making observations like "he's always in the right place at the right time," or "she's just a natural, one in a million," or "with connections like theirs, who needs talent?" But what if there is more to the story than simply having the right timing, the right stuff or the right friends?

Energy is the driving force behind all aspects of our lives. Light, heat, electricity, sound, thought, movement, and even physical substance are some of the common forms that energy takes as it plays within our everyday processes and experiences. Our minds and bodies function by absorbing and/or managing these various forms of energy in order to maintain our health, fuel our actions, and fulfill our intentions.

The energy that you command at any given moment might be thought of as your *personal power*. This is the life-force that drives your being, the raw material for all of your activities. Through it, you live, love, learn, and create.

For many of us, a majority of our personal power is devoured each day by mental, behavioral, and biological processes that run nonstop inside us. Rather than learning to *intentionally* command our own energies, we develop routine outlets that vent them almost as quickly as they are absorbed. Consider several common examples:

3

- We engross ourselves in a relentless flow of duties, activities, and projects, many of which are repetitive and lackluster.

- We labor to convert our energies into money and simultaneously develop the habitual urge to "spend" that money, often frivolously; we soon find ourselves indebted to others.

- We medicate ourselves with various substances, indulge in heavy foods, and engage in distracting media, binding our energies to these highly consuming processes.

- We "over-think" and "rationalize" our power into intellectual submission, imprisoning it in contemplation rather than using it to take action.

- We burn up our energies by pitting them against one another through internal struggle or against the energies of other people through often needless competitions and conflicts.

- We organize the activities of weekly life into tight schedules, the folly of which becomes apparent with a subtle stirring of anxiety around dinner time Sunday night as we prepare for the consuming demands of the weekdays ahead.

Powerful people tend to avoid pitfalls like these. They do not necessarily have more inherent power than anyone else. They simply avoid squandering that which they do have, thus freeing it up for more productive uses. As a result they are generally healthy and appealing, regardless of physical features. They have *that certain something*, carrying themselves with notable presence. They are clear and focused, and things seem to go their way with apparently little effort. They know how to accumulate energy and therefore tend to hold a plentiful reserve.

How many among us wish they had more energy and enthusiasm to power them through their days? How many commonly find themselves feeling drained to the point that they've got little if any energy left for things they most care about in life?

Empowerment is the art of managing your personal power. By learning to direct your energies effectively and efficiently, extraordinary feats become possible, and even commonplace. An inner wellspring of energy soon lights your path, and matters like low self-esteem or hopelessness fade away.

For one interested in truly harnessing his or her personal power, or in helping others to do the same, three topics are of value:

1. **The Nature of Energy**—Understanding how energy acts within your life.

2. **Personal Power**—Understanding your life-force and recognizing how habitual behaviors squander much of this vital energy.

3. **Developing Empowerment**—Learning to regain conscious command of your own personal power.

The Nature of Energy

Have you ever found yourself lying in bed, waiting for the alarm clock to sound, all the while feeling an uncomfortable sense of dread? Perhaps you're already half-awake, but it's hard to imagine leaving the coziness and warmth beneath your sheets just yet. Something feels instinctively wrong about the mere prospect of it, of having to start your day before fully gathering the will to do so.

What does it take to find yourself exuberantly tossing the sheets away each morning ready for action, feeling excited to go after whatever it is that your new day holds for you? What does it take to truly *spend* a day, to give it all you've got, and yet hit the sheets at night feeling as empowered or even more so than when your day began? What does it take to tackle a seemingly insurmountable obstacle, or to realize a dream, or to simply have a dream in the first place?

It takes *energy*.

Energy is the underlying form of all things. Of dreams. Of actions. Of attitudes. Of accomplishments. Even physical substance is composed of energy, as described by Albert Einstein's famous formula $E=mc^2$, which relates the mass, "m," of a given substance to its underlying energy, "E." Every object, every being, every thought, every activity and every relationship results from the flow and interaction of energies.

To understand the mysterious dance that energy performs as it flows through our universe, consider a common example of its transformational behavior in our everyday lives.

Picture the sun shining brightly at the center of our solar system. It is a large ball of physical substance like our planet, composed primarily of the elements hydrogen and helium. Intense reactions in the sun's photosphere transform some of the *chemical energy* bound in hydrogen to a different form of energy known as *sunlight*. Once released from the tight confines of physical substance, this energy is free to travel off through the universe at 670,616,629 miles per hour.

Some sunlight enters Earth's atmosphere where it is absorbed and transformed once again into other forms of energy. For example, plants convert sunlight back into physical substance. Special biological molecules called *proteins* are responsible for capturing the light energy once it enters a plant cell; they transform it back into chemical energy—commonly, into forms such as *sugar* or *carbohydrate*. If you eat the plant, this energy becomes available to you and your various activities. In a sense, you are eating sunlight.

Proteins are the workers inside all living cells, both plant and animal. Their job is to convert energies from one form to another. Some proteins create sugars and carbohydrates. Some use energy to manufacture other organic substances such as fat, D.N.A., body tissues or new proteins. Some convert chemical energy into heat, movement, and so on.

When you get out of bed in the morning, your intelligence uses *electrical energy* to tell your various muscles what to do. Proteins in those muscles instantly draw upon *chemical energy* to get you moving onto your feet, then off to the kitchen or bathroom. Similarly, proteins in your heart muscles use chemical energy to pump blood and nutrients throughout your body, providing all your cells and tissues with the raw materials they need to perform their various functions.

Every moment of your life, your body is converting an unfathomable number of energies from one form to another in order to carry out your various functions and activities. The art of empowerment is the art of increasing your efficiency in using the immense energy available to you. It is based upon four energetic principles that pertain to everyday life:

Energy takes many forms, each exhibiting different properties.

Chemical energy is bound in physical substances such as body tissues, oxygen, food and water; its flow is tightly confined inside atoms and molecules. *Electrical energy* flows through the nervous system in a manner less densely confined than chemical energy, yet highly organized. *Electromagnetic energies* such as light and heat are radiant, moving more freely about. *Kinetic energy* flows through movements large and small—such as an athlete sprinting across a field or tiny bones in the ear vibrating to produce hearing. Regardless of form, energies are always in motion, always flowing about.

Energy can be converted from one form to another, but is neither created nor destroyed.

From sunlight to sugar, and from sugar to a world record sprint, energies are constantly transmuted from one form to another, changing disguise as they flow about through the universe to yield the phenomena of everyday life. They are never simply created out of thin air, however, and never put to rest.

Living beings function by absorbing, manipulating and releasing various forms of energy.

The body is a kind of *energetic field*—an extraordinary array of organized, overlapping energies. Some of these energies are quite dense and solid, while others are subtler. When you breathe, drink, and eat, you absorb dense chemical energies into your energetic field, fueling your physical body and its various biological processes. Sensory organs and other body components absorb *subtler* energies, fueling your mind and consciousness. Once absorbed, any form of energy can be used and manipulated. Eventually you release it back out to the world in a number of different forms: through action, movement, warmth, emotion, communication, excretion, and so forth.

Intelligence operates by directing the flow and conversion of energies.

Living beings use intelligence to control their activities and to bring form to themselves and the world around them. There are two primary forms of intelligence, *mechanical* and *conscious,* each of which harnesses and manipulates energies in different ways. **Mechanical intelligence** directs the flow and transformation of energies *automatically*. For example: At the cellular level, proteins perform various repetitive jobs, directing energy in a manner that fulfills specific genetic instructions; at the neurological level, reflexes and electrical pathways direct energy through automated channels, influencing our habits and behaviors; at the technological level, devices perform activities that automate the flow and conversion of energies. Much of the intelligence exhibited on Earth is mechanical in nature. In contrast, *conscious intelligence* uses *attention* to direct the flow and conversion of energy. Unlike mechanical intelligence, it learns from its own activities, adapting and improving its methods for manipulating energy through each new experience. Thought, intention, and creativity are common examples of this more complex form of intelligence.

Energy is the substance of life, the medium through which one sculpts his or her being. The more that one's energy is directed mechanically—automatically—the less it is available for conscious control. As we will see in the next section, most of us have an overabundance of mechanical intelligence running all day long that burns through our energies. We can therefore be left with relatively little free energy for truly powerful action.

By learning to consciously harness the energy available within and around us, we *empower* ourselves to participate more fully in the art of life, in the ongoing art of self-development.

Personal Power

The sum total of your available energy can be thought of as *personal power*. Many everyday activities tend to expend this vital energy as quickly as it is absorbed. However, you can learn to reduce your spending, thereby accumulating a reserve of energy known as *will*, which is the fuel of conscious action. Will is essential to a number of activities including health, free choice, success, and the fulfillment of intentions.

As with money, there is an art to budgeting personal power. Financially wealthy people are not necessarily the ones with the highest paying jobs. They often simply employ keen strategies that allow them to capitalize on whatever income is available to them. Similarly, anyone can learn to gather a nest-egg of free will by reducing the automated waste of vital energy. That which is not spent becomes immediately available for more empowering activities.

There are several general pathways through which we mismanage the flow of personal power, leaving ourselves with relatively little free will:

Routines

Human beings, like all animals, develop routine behaviors as a means of conserving energy. These behaviors allow us to use energy in a skilled and efficient manner. Unfortunately, we tend to overuse them, and in doing so, route much of our personal power through highly repetitive acts such as morning habits, evening habits, weekend habits, work habits, eating habits, and so on. To compound matters, many of us over-program our lives by taking on more responsibilities than we can manage and schedule a day's energy usage weeks or months before-hand, sometimes down to the hour and minute. Over time we feel a growing need for a vacation, or more accurately, an instinctive yearning to liberate personal power from the consuming demands of our excessive everyday routines. Many athletes, artists, and entrepreneurs do not live their lives confined to such routines and instead wield their personal power more freely and dynamically.

Outlets

Children are often admired for their energetic exuberance, yet adults commonly feel uncomfortable around this youthful expression of personal power. Anxious or annoyed, we teach children to vent their abundant energies through outlets that we deem "appropriate," such as activities, sports, hobbies, and studies. When we do this, we rob children of daily opportunities for regulating and managing their own energies. By adolescence many young people begin to fear excess accumulations of their own power. They learn to rely on outlets to vent it quickly and effectively. By adulthood this venting process becomes automatic. Although certain "outlet" activities can be healthy and even productive, the underlying fear of personal power and the need to "let it out" is an energetically self-sabotaging endeavor. If we learn to identify our outlets we may then distinguish the productive ones from the energetic drains.

Addictions

Rather than consciously managing our energies, we sometimes use substances or situations to manage them for us. Caffeine, alcohol, drugs, overeating, over-exercise, pornography, television, video games, and other media are common forms that we typically use to automatically route our energies when we are unsure of how to direct them ourselves. It is not necessarily the substance or activity itself that squanders our power, but rather our addictive reliance upon it to direct our energies for us. *Intentional boredom* can be an excellent antidote, allowing us to sit quietly with our power for a time. Soon that power finds fresh, creative ways to flow.

Hemorrhages

As the years pass, we tend to develop power leakages, unwittingly venting energy without awareness. Common forms of hemorrhages include whining, complaining, gossiping, or nit-picking about ourselves and others; judging, fearing, resisting, or resenting certain circumstances; wallowing in our feelings by indulging, obsessing, and feeling sorry for ourselves or others. Each form of hemorrhage causes us to leak energy without growth or progress. Self-limiting beliefs have a similar effect. They arise when we hold onto sad stories from the past, carrying them around with us as if they are truths of the present. All the while, we vent power through a sense of lacking or misfortune. Another common hemorrhage is the pouring of one's energy into relationships without concern for health or balance. This attracts social embezzlers who take what they can get, then move on, eventually uncomfortable with their own degree of energetic vampirism. By learning to plug our leaks we conserve this otherwise wasted power.

Commercialism

Money is one of the more unusual forms that energy takes, representing our purchase power for human labor and natural resources. Thanks to the tremendous energy that money enables us to access, *money fixation* has become an ordinary stage of a young citizen's development. We learn to invest much of our personal power into making it, spending it, fantasizing about it, cheating other people out of it, or gambling for it. In the ideal, money serves to balance people's civic cooperation. In reality, most of us tend to put far more energy into it than we get out of it. If we learn to spend less, we then need less.

Repression

We sometimes force ourselves to store emotional energies such as distress, anxiety, and tension. We then establish charges in our energetic fields that block the clean flow of personal power. Unreleased or unprocessed, these charges accumulate, counteracting and consuming our energies. Not only do they decrease the efficiency of our energy usage; they also encourage addictive behaviors. Over time they may even yield physical illness or disease such as back pain, heart conditions, and other serious ailments. Various health disciplines such as yoga, acupuncture, and other therapies or practices help to release these antithetical energies with a minimal expenditure of personal power. Chapter 2 will explore several powerful mechanisms for clearing this emotional charge.

Egotism

I want. *I* need. *I* this. *I* that. Self-absorption causes us to waste vast amounts of personal power on our image and self-importance, generally at the expense of personal growth. This topic will be examined more closely in Chapter 6: The Art of Authenticity.

Combined, these seven forms of mismanagement consume immense amounts of personal power, yielding a kind of energetic bankruptcy that may surface in the form of tiredness, carelessness, apathy, numbness, discouragement, sadness, hopelessness, depression, cold-heartedness, aging, illness, or accident-prone behavior. In most cases, however, the misuse of personal power simply causes us to harness less of the extraordinary potential and vitality available to us each moment of every day.

Writer Alice Walker once said, "The most common way people give up their power is by thinking they don't have any." When all of one's incoming energy is automatically spent on habitual behaviors that are never questioned or even noticed, it is easy to draw the assumption that he or she is simply, inherently powerless.

By learning to curtail our various forms of frivolous energetic spending, we begin to liberate excess personal power, or *will*, which becomes available for pursuits such as creating, loving, learning, healing, realizing, and ultimately, evolving.

From generation to generation, adults hand down the seven habitual mechanisms examined earlier, limiting the will and therefore the life potential of the common youth. Fortunately this phenomenon can be reversed at any age through the art of empowerment.

Developing Empowerment

Imagine a bachelor named Bernard, who runs every device in his home 24 hours a day. He leaves on all the lights, both computers, several TVs, as well as radios, media players, fans, heaters, air conditioning, washer and dryer, both refrigerators, kitchen and bathroom appliances, showers, faucets, gardening equipment, his car, and a motorcycle.

As one might expect, Bernard's monthly utility bill is outrageously high, consuming a majority of his income. This leaves him with only a small reserve of money for food, healthcare, and clothing, and absolutely no money for dating, travel, recreation, cultural activities, hobbies, schooling, or altruism. With a full-time day job and a second night job, there is little time for such activities anyway.

One evening, quite out of the blue, Bernard makes a grand discovery. He notices a funny little object sticking out of the wall. As he fiddles with it, the garbage disposal grinds to a halt. He flips another one of these strange objects and the kitchen lights go out. It is in this moment that Bernard stumbles upon the concept of *on-versus-off*. Tickled by the novelty of it, he dashes about the house turning off every appliance that is not immediately necessary. His home suddenly becomes quiet, peaceful, easing.

A month later, Bernard's utility bill arrives 93% lower than ever before. Within three months, a significant surplus of money amasses in his bank account. He promptly quits his night job, at which time new interests and inspirations ignite within him—sparked by the gift of free time. In pursuing them, he finds himself encountering people and opportunities that had previously seemed beyond his grasp. It is as if an entirely new life, new world and new possibilities unfold before his very eyes, unearthed by his accumulating means.

Empowerment, much like Bernard's grand discovery, is the art of turning off all the unnecessary appliances in one's being in order to liberate energy for more intentional uses. One begins to gather a reserve of personal power, or *will*, which can then be applied to a wide range of exciting pursuits including personal growth.

By halting the various mechanisms that squander our energies, engaging instead in activities that focus and accumulate these energies, we find the fuel to awaken that great potential dormant within—a potential that might otherwise seem beyond our reach.

At the outset of empowering one's self, the novice has relatively little *will* available. He or she faces an immediate stumbling block, in that will is not simply the *product* of empowerment; it is also the *primary resource* used in developing it. As with money, the more you have to invest, the greater your return.

Consider the case of someone who wishes to quit an addiction. To accomplish this feat a base supply of willpower is essential. Yet the addiction consumes most if not all of the addict's free personal power. As a result, he or she lacks the will necessary to break the habit.

Similarly, the average person is hooked on hundreds of subtle routines. None of them are as flagrantly apparent as a major addiction yet, when combined, these subtle vents of power leave him or her much like the addict—operating with only a fraction of the will available to him or her.

The first step in empowering yourself is to liberate an initial supply of will, which can then be applied to furthering the art, in turn liberating more will, and so on. The process unfolds slowly, one little act at a time. Each shift in behavior breeds further shifts. The more free will you accumulate, the easier it is to set up your life in a manner that allows you to accumulate yet more of this vital energy.

A wide spread of techniques can be used for developing personal empowerment. The following seven techniques serve as the founding essentials, liberating that initial reserve of power for other, more advanced techniques:

[1] The Intentional Breath

Through the natural course of each day, challenges arise, including conflicts, emotional outbursts, anxieties, tensions, and unexpected situations or circumstances. These conditions sometimes channel our energies in non-productive ways that cause our own power to work against us or against those around us. A few slow, deep breaths in through the nose and out through the mouth can reset our circuits, allowing us to reengage with refreshed clarity. Simply inhale *slowly and deeply* through your nose as you imagine the oxygen infusing every cell in your body. In turn, exhale *slowly and deeply* through your mouth, imagining emotion or unfavorable energy released to a place that will refresh it. This intentional breath is an innate reset switch. It is so powerful that it can turn your entire day around in ninety seconds.

[2] DISCIPLINE (A.K.A. EXCELLENCE)

Just as a lens is used to focus light, self-discipline is used to focus personal power. It doesn't matter what you focus on, so long as you give it your all. You can peel potatoes, clean the bathroom, practice a desired skill, pay attention to someone or something, pray, play, or create. By focusing 100% on the task at hand to give it everything you've got, you shut down the multitude of routine vents that otherwise scatter your power. In this way, not only do you perform a high quality job on the task at hand, but you gain energy in the process that might otherwise have been wastefully spent. *By focusing completely on a single, pure act, you allow yourself to become temporarily extraordinary*. Great athletes, artists, and entrepreneurs are not always powerful right out of the womb or powerful as the result of good fortune or privilege. Many accumulate their power through the disciplined pursuit of their sport, art, or enterprise. They cultivate their *will* while cultivating their craft.

[3] ADVENTURE

A fairly easy way to liberate power is to cut a basic routine from your day, taking the opportunity to think or behave in a manner that is fresh and new. Your adventure need not be extravagant. You can simply alter the steps in bathing, take a different route to work, go somewhere out of the ordinary, or have an unusual meal. Each spontaneous act draws you into the present moment, freeing up a little personal power. You may notice an increase in your energy level through a feeling of excitement, courage, or adventurousness. The trick is to keep these adventures *spontaneous* by avoiding the tendency to habituate them into new routines. The example in Exercise 3b on page 56 outlines a way to develop this quality.

[4] ATTITUDE

The mind is like a switchboard that directs the flow of life energy. It has certain general settings called *attitudes* or *moods*. When in a humorous mood our energy is directed to flow in a free, light-hearted manner through smiles, giggles, and laughter. Other common attitudes include courage, compassion, playfulness, persistence, frustration, resistance, arrogance, and greed. Each directs one's personal power to flow in a unique way, bringing about specific feelings and behaviors. We can summon any attitude at will by simply thinking about it, focusing attention on the qualities and feelings that correspond with it. In doing so, we mentally reconfigure the flow of our energies. A bad mood can only last as long as one allows energy to be directed to it. As an example, try to imagine a feeling of *compassion*. Think of someone you love in a moment when he or she is hurt. Feel this attitude flowing through your whole body, affecting your posture, facial expressions, behavior, and thoughts. Imagine your compassion flowing in waves, filling that person with your love and support. Now allow yourself to redirect this compassion toward someone you dislike. Be courageous and powerful about it. *Will* the attitude into being, and then wield it masterfully.

[5] PATIENCE

In the art of empowerment, timing is everything. The effectiveness of our actions can be influenced heavily by the conditions at hand. Under *advantageous* conditions, success is achieved using relatively little personal power. Far more power is consumed under unfavorable conditions. By learning to wait patiently, accumulating energy all the while, we develop the ability to leap into action spryly and deliberately when the right opportunity arises. Situations, like life, unfold in mysterious rhythms. By waiting for the proper tide, even a massive vessel can be launched with relatively minimal effort.

[6] MASTERY

By working to master a skill or talent, one learns to channel energy with great cunning and precision. In baseball, for example, an expert batter coordinates the movement of muscles and joints in a manner that maximizes the transfer of power to the ball and directs its course with pinpoint accuracy. By contrast, a novice batter expends more energy on the same act with significantly weaker results. Through disciplined study, one can develop command over a wide range of activities including athletics, intellectual pursuits, arts, languages, crafts, hobbies, talents, professions, social skills, politics, diplomacy, and so on. The wider one's spread of mastered skills, the more efficient his or her usage of personal power day in and day out.

[7] CONDITIONING

Nutrition, sleep, and exercise are the building-blocks of everyday vitality, keeping the flow of our bioenergies free and healthy. Together they form a power-trio, each supporting the others. Regular *exercise* tends to promote deep sleep while stimulating cravings for healthy foods. Good *nutrition* optimizes regeneration during sleep and fuels one for healthy exercise. A full night's *sleep* gives both the body and mind ample time to process energies absorbed during the day. Prioritizing these activities in our lifestyles creates a condition of health that others can't help but notice. Disciplines such as athletics, yoga, or martial arts help to support both physical and mental conditioning, and can liberate a healthy supply of will in the process.

These seven techniques serve as the fundamental tools of empowerment. They allow you to become more consciously aware of how your energy is spent, to gain some control in managing it, and to increase your reserve of free will. If you engage in Exercise 1a on page 19 you should notice a boost in your level of willpower within a week or two. You may feel more energized, healthy, confident, or self-aware. You can then begin to apply this growing accumulation of will to more advanced techniques, reinvesting your dividends into the further development of empowerment. *Each of the chapters in this book presents an advanced art for building and maintaining personal power.*

The following story provides an example of how just a few of these techniques can help jump-start a fresh approach to life at any age, awakening and revitalizing your innermost cares, dreams and ambitions.

It is a warm June afternoon. An 86-year-old woman steps up to the podium at her college graduation, charmed by a roar of applause. She shakes hands with the chancellor of the university and then graciously accepts a beautifully crafted rosewood plaque—the first annual *Shining Spirit Award*. Smiling warmly at the crowd, she begins to speak.

"People often ask me how I managed to have a second start so late in life. I suppose the truth isn't as glamorous as I'd like it to be. Things just happened one little step at a time. And now here I am, the oldest woman ever to receive a bachelor's degree from this university.

"I was recently thumbing through my old diaries and found six entries that seem to capture the early steps that led me here. I've shared them with the chancellor, and he's asked me to share them with you today. So here goes.

"*August 25, 2003*. Hi Sweetie. My new prescription comes in tomorrow. I'll pick it up late afternoon after the soap operas. Then sometime tomorrow night, I'll work my way through the whole bottle. That ought to do the trick. And after six long months, we'll finally be together once again. I hope you don't meet me with disapproval. I miss you so. Ever since you passed, I've felt the life draining from my bones. I mope around the apartment day and night. I've got nothing left. I'll see you tomorrow, Sweetie.

"*August 26, 2003*. Hi Sweetie. I realize that it's after 9:00 p.m. and I'm still not with you. I had an unusual day. You know those gorgeous roses outside our bedroom window? When I woke up this morning and saw them swaying there in the breeze, I thought about how this was going to be the last day of my life. I realized how fortunate I was, not having to spend it in a hospital bed, unlike some people we know. I wondered how you would have spent your last day if you'd had your health. Right away, I thought of the airport and that introductory pilot's flight you always talked about. Within a few hours I was signed up for a private lesson. I found myself boarding a cute little single-propeller plane as the surrogate for your last hurrah. I even flew it for a time. Then I threw up, and it was back to the airport with me. This was the best day I've had since kissing you goodnight that final time. It slipped my mind to pick up the pills after all that. I guess we'll just have to wait one more night for our reunion. That'll give me a chance to have my own last hurrah. I wonder what I'll do. See you tomorrow, Sweetie.

"*August 27, 2003*. Hi Sweetie. Remember that yoga thing they used to do in the 70s? And how I was always talking about wanting to try it? And how you and the boys always teased me to shame about it? Well, I found a beginner's class in town this afternoon. I marched right down there. Ordinarily I might have nagged and complained the whole time through. They make you sit on the floor. But remembering that this was my grand, final hurrah, I decided to pretend that I was having the best time ever. In truth, yoga is quite invigorating. My poor, lazy foot perked right up. Afterwards I drove past the hospital one last time thinking of you, thinking of our time together there. A concessionaire was selling beautifully potted flowers out front. It made me think of how dismal your room had been. Then something came over me. I parked the car, bought a couple potted flowers and snuck into your old wing on the second floor. I spied two lonely patients, so sad and lifeless. I brought each of them a flower. And Sweetie, you should have seen their faces. I'm gonna stick around one more day so I can cut some of our beautiful roses and deliver them to a few more patients. Then I'll see you tomorrow night.

"*August 28, 2003*. Hi Babe. I realize that you might find humor in the irony of all this. Somehow the daily prospect of my own death is like a good, stiff shot in the tush. Instead of ending me, it's bringing me back to life. I figure if I've only got a few hours left, I had better make them count. Right? So it's the invigoration of yoga instead of the scandal and tragedy in my soaps. It's flowers for people who really need them rather than cards and hard lemonade with the girls. It would seem that on this— yet another last day of my life—death hasn't come for me just yet. Maybe it'll be tomorrow, Sweetie.

"*August 29, 2003*. You won't believe what happened today. I brought some flowers to a woman who seemed to really need them. She was at a loss when I gave them to her and began to sob. Apparently the doctors had removed her plumbing the day before. No more babies for her. She couldn't stop thanking me for dropping in and listening to her. My visit meant so much. Then she and I got to talking. She suggested that we turn my little flower operation into a nonprofit corporation! We're thinking of calling it: *Hope's in Bloom*. Isn't that great? I have to tell you, I'm feeling a little nervous about it. I've never tried to start a corporation before. Anyway, I know one of these days too soon will be my last. Maybe it'll be tomorrow, Sweetie.

"*August 30, 2003*. Hi Hank. I've been thinking about something. I figure, if I'm gonna be the cofounder of a volunteer organization, and the gray queen of the yoga studio, then what's to keep me from going to college? I know how you always felt about that. As *you* know, it's been a lifelong dream of mine. Perhaps I can't earn an entire bachelors degree in a single day, but at least I can drop by the admissions office. I hope you're as proud of me as I am of myself. Maybe I'll see you tomorrow, Sweetie."

Success in any endeavor is dependent upon the manner in which we use the resources and energies available to us. The single greatest cause of human limitation is a lack of personal power, or more accurately, the gross misuse of available energy. By sorting through the behaviors and routines of everyday life—differentiating those that are empowering from those that are depleting—one can craft a lifestyle that nourishes the highest potential available within.

Chapter 7, "The Art of Actualization," will explore the technique of *setting intentions* as a means of applying one's will directly toward actualizing something—making it happen. It can be used to master skills, build relationships, heal illnesses, fulfill dreams, or bring about transformations. The greater one's accumulation of *will*, the greater the volition with which intentions are fueled and therefore achieved.

The various techniques of empowerment allow us to accumulate this abundance of energy. They can be applied not only to one's self, but to a relationship, to a family, to a community or even a society. Thomas Jefferson, third U.S. president and author of its Declaration of Independence once said, "I hope our wisdom will grow with our power, and teach us that the less we use our power, the greater it will be."

The excellence and efficiency of any nation or of our global community at large is driven by the collective empowerment of individuals. Gross consumer waste, haphazard bureaucratic spending, and the careless consumption of natural resources are all reflections of the mismanagement of personal power common within the average citizen.

In the big picture empowerment is not only a means of personal development. It is a key that opens billions of doorways to societal progress.

Chapter 1 Exercises

Exercise 1a: Developing Personal Power

Read through the empowerment techniques once again on pages 13-16. This will help to deepen your understanding before you proceed with the exercise. Next, analyze the story on page 16. *Which techniques did the elderly woman use to empower herself?* Your analysis will help you to better understand the techniques of empowerment in action.

Now consider your own life circumstances. Which of the seven techniques appeal to you as useful methods of empowerment? Pick one. Read through the description of it one more time and analyze it in the context of your own life. *Do you know of anyone who uses this technique effectively?* Talk to him or her about it. If not, imagine a master of the technique and how he or she might use it.

Once you have chosen a technique that most resonates with your personality, think about when and how you can use it in your everyday life. Consider situations where it may be of value, or ways that you might apply it today, tonight or tomorrow. Choose applications that you believe you can *successfully* accomplish. Make a simple list of them. Then imagine yourself going through each application. Imagination is a very powerful form of practice.

Finally, set out to use your chosen technique as much as possible in the next 24 hours. Realize that the more energy you put into it, the more energy you will get out of it. By the end of tomorrow night, go through your list and check off all the applications that you actually used. Add any new ones that you may have developed during the day. Ponder how the various applications went and what you might do differently tomorrow to make them more effective. Be sure to appreciate and celebrate your efforts, large or small.

Repeat this reflection process every day. If you really apply yourself, you should notice a boost in your energy or sense of empowerment within a week or two. You will also establish this technique as a regular activity in your repertoire, available to you every day. You may now choose a new technique to develop, or apply your energy to one of the more advanced empowerment arts explored throughout the other chapters. Alternatively, you can go on to Exercise 1b.

To download a workbook that corresponds with this chapter, take a look at page 184: *User's Guide* Support Materials.

Exercise 1b: Shutting Down the Waste of Personal Power

Read through the list of the common vents of power on pages 9-11. Think of the top three categories in which you most frequently vent your power. You might select *Routines, Outlets, Addictions, Hemorrhages, Commercialism, Repression,* or *Egotism*. Read the descriptions of these three noticeable ways in which you vent power several times through, considering specific examples of how they play out in your own life. Be honest with yourself. List the typical ways you waste your power in each type of vent, noting the most common examples that affect you daily and weekly.

Now choose *one* of these top three power vents—the one you most wish to reduce. *What measures might you take to accomplish this goal?*

Consider the empowerment techniques on pages 13-16. Can any of them help you seal this particular energy leakage? Try to think of someone who avoids venting power in this manner. *What is it about their behavior that makes this possible?* Write down all the possible things you might try in order to seal this vent in yourself.

Set out in the next 24 hours to conserve your power by using some or all of the methods you listed. Begin by imagining the use of each method in an actual circumstance where you might otherwise vent power. The more energy you put into your efforts, the more effective you will be.

By the end of tomorrow night go through your list and check off the methods you actually used. Add new ones that you may have developed along the way. Ponder your successes and failures throughout the day, and what you might do differently the next day to be more effective. Realize that failures are every bit as valuable as successes since they offer insights about your challenges and weaknesses. Set out courageously to learn from them.

Repeat this 5-minute reflection process every night. If you really apply yourself, you will begin to feel an increasing command over your own power within two weeks and will find yourself gaining energy in the process. You may now choose a different vent of power to reduce or return to Exercise 1a.

Empowerment is a state of self-mastery, a cunning use of personal power. Vigilance is essential to the art, as old habits and routines are always on the prowl waiting to take back the power that temporarily was theirs. Set a clear intention, such as *I am master of my own power,* or *I use my energy wisely and intentionally.* Restate your intention frequently each day. One little step at a time, you will make it true.

Essential Questions

Take a few moments to ponder the following questions. Allow your-self to come up with at least three answers to each question as a means of self-discovery. Keep a written record of your answers in a log or journal.

- How do my hurts, fears, sorrows and frustrations express themselves?

- How does my brilliance express itself? *(What are my greatest skills, talents or aptitudes?)*

- What might it take to live more fully in my *brilliance*, not in my *distress*?

CHAPTER 2

The Art of Brilliance

*What a distressing contrast there is between the radiant intelligence
of the child and the feeble mentality of the average adult.*

—SIGMUND FREUD, neurologist and psychologist (1856–1939)

Why is it that young children are generally so creative and imaginative in the ways that they approach play, love, life, and even the most mundane activities? Why is it that many adults feel they lack creativity, or imagination, or both of these natural human attributes? How is it that 4-year-olds so cleverly find ways to get what they want while their parents often struggle to simply keep what they have? What is it that allows kindergartners to learn from their mistakes while college graduates often make the same mistakes over and over again?

We often think of *brilliance* as a rare quality reserved for a few, special people. Perhaps this is because we are largely unaware of the extraordinary intellectual capacities that we exhibit early on in life. By the time we are old enough to appreciate them, these capacities usually seem to have diminished. This is not the result of aging or deterioration, however, as much as the improper *care* of intelligence. In other words, "the feeble mentality of the average adult" described by Freud is mostly a matter of poor intellectual maintenance. It can be reversed.

Intelligence naturally tends to advance itself from one moment to the next, allowing us to continually improve the quality of our lives. *Brilliance* is its most free-flowing state, a radiant and dynamic use of the intelligence available to us. Though each person expresses it differently, brilliance allows us to learn rapidly and to use any situation as an opportunity for growth.

Many U.S. high school graduates complete their standard years of schooling without ever directly learning about a single aspect of intelligence—what it is, how it functions, or how to care for it. Just as a driver is well served to understand the basic aspects of an automobile in order to optimize its performance, each person should have a basic understanding of intelligence in order to effectively operate his or her *self*, and therein to make the most of life.

By learning to nourish and cleanse your intelligence, you enable yourself to proceed from day to day with brilliance and power. Attending to your own intellectual maintenance, you avoid that "feeble mentality" so prevalent among teens and adults everywhere.

To accomplish this, consider the following three topics:

1. **The Nature of Intelligence**—Recognizing what intelligence is and how it functions.

2. **Nourishing Your Intelligence**—Learning how to invigorate and expand your intelligence.

3. **Awakening Your Own Brilliance**—Learning to maintain a state of intellectual radiance through proper emotional care.

The Nature of Intelligence

People often think of intelligence in terms of how "smart" they are, or how well they do in school, or how quickly and deeply they are able to think things through. Yet when it comes right down to it, few people can actually tell you what intelligence really is. They figure that they were born with a set amount of it, whatever the heck it is, so what's the point in pondering it?

The point is that we are *not* born with a set amount of it. Moreover, intelligence is the machinery that drives our ongoing growth and well-being. It powers our actions and dreams. It directs our work, play, love, and relationships. It shapes the people that we become year after year, decade after decade. As such, it is a matter worth pondering.

Intelligence is simply a capacity that controls the flow and use of energy. In human beings, it acts by directing our personal power. It is often thought of as existing inside the brain, but it actually runs throughout the entire body. By commanding our various forms of energy—electrical, chemical, kinetic and so on—intelligence controls everything we do.

The microscopic cells throughout our body tissues and organs exhibit what might be thought of as *mechanical intelligence*, which was described in Chapter 1 on page 7. This form of intelligence directs energy through basic, automatic functions such as manufacturing various substances, creating movement, and carrying out habitual behaviors. All are basic, repetitive acts that automatically direct the flow of our energies.

By contrast, *conscious intelligence* operates creatively, considering a wide range of possibilities when choosing how best to act. It uses our *attention* to focus and control the flow of energies both within and around us. Yours is currently busy comprehending this paragraph.

Take a moment to really think about the extraordinary activities that your intelligence is involved in at this very instant. For example, if you are visually reading these sentences, light energy is radiating into your eyes, carrying with it complex information from the page. This information is then converted into electrical impulses and transmitted to your brain. This is an absorption of energy into your intelligence, an input of information into your mind's eye.

Meanwhile, your intelligence uses energy to control the various muscles in and around your eyes. It instructs them to focus your sights on the page, to track the words from left to right, and to occasionally blink in order to refresh the eyes. It is in constant communication with your various eye muscles, coordinating their efforts with its own. In this manner, it manipulates energies throughout your body. It controls everything you do.

Once your intelligence receives the information from this page, it begins to process it. Like a linguist consulting a dictionary, it consults an intellectual library deep within you—the warehouse of everything you have learned. Words and phrases on the page are matched with information already on file in your memory. You quickly make sense of these sentences, stringing the words together into ideas. You ponder the ideas, cross-reference them with your own understandings about things, and continue onward through the text. This all takes place at an astonishing speed—regardless of how smart you believe you are.

Meanwhile this information and all your related thoughts about it are rapidly sorted and filed in your intellectual library. Through the process, the inner library of everything you know continually expands and reorganizes itself. You become consistently smarter.

If you decide to speak these words aloud, your intelligence directs energy through your lungs, vocal cords, and mouth to create highly specialized vibrations, also known as *spoken words*. The energy travels through the air in waves of sound. If these waves hit a listener's ears, an energy conversion process begins all over again as your listener inputs the energy. It is in this way that you communicate with other conscious beings out there in the world; you send and receive energies in various forms, including sounds, movements, gestures and touch.

Imagine now that you are a high school student reading these words aloud in class. Imagine that you are suddenly asked by your teacher to explain what "intelligence" is. Perhaps you find yourself swallowing awkwardly, feeling put on the spot. Other students begin to laugh. A sense of distress arises inside you, temporarily overwhelming your conscious intelligence. You too may begin to laugh or feel tears warming your eyes. These are natural attempts by your intelligence to release this disruptive overload of energy, to cleanse you of your distress.

Fearing chastisement from your teacher or peers, you may choose to repress the emotion, downloading your distress directly into your intelligence rather than releasing it. In doing this you fog up your intelligence just a little bit, blurring the line between thoughts and feelings, recording them side by side.

Ultimately, conscious intelligence enables us to *learn* and to then apply our learning toward *action*. In the process of reading these various paragraphs you may find yourself considering the proposition that intelligence is not a fixed thing, that you were not born with a set amount of it. You may recognize that the more effort you put into developing it, the stronger it becomes. You now have the opportunity to apply your learning toward some action. For example, you may choose to read on, exploring the art of how to nourish your intelligence, or how to keep it clean and radiant.

Of the four key activities that your intelligence engages in—*communicating, processing, storing,* and *emoting* various forms of energy—the *storing* of energetic information is the easiest one to measure, should you ever feel the compulsion to do so. You can fill your intellectual library with basic facts and skills. Then you can test it quite simply by using multiple-choice questionnaires. For this reason school systems often find that it is the most satisfying component of your intelligence to *educate.*

Consider what happens when a society focuses its schooling practices on the storing of information in your intellectual library—just one of four components in your intelligence—but neglects nurturing your overall intelligence. Lots of facts may be memorized, but you do not necessarily learn to understand or communicate these facts with much sophistication. Nor do you necessarily learn what to do with them or how to feel about them.

Today, almost any important fact can be pulled off the internet in five minutes. Because society has evolved, it is no longer appropriate to so heavily emphasize *memorization* in education. It is far more critical that you learn to nourish, develop, and maintain your intelligence in its totality, supporting your innate brilliance in every thought and action.

Nourishing Your Intelligence

When I was thirteen years old, my mom sat me down and asked, "Honey, do you have any questions about sex?"

I stared at her in horror, then quickly replied, "Um, no."

I had countless questions, of course, but I wanted to discuss them with someone who might understand first-hand all the weird things that I was experiencing as an adolescent boy.

The following week Mom brought me to our family pediatrician. Dr. Hill met with me and two other under-informed boys to give us the scoop on sex. Using diagrams and flow charts, we learned about tubes, glands, organs, and various substances, each with very clinical sounding names. He offered loads of information about the reproductive system. Then he sent us home with some pamphlets for further reading.

I walked out of the office feeling completely disappointed. I'd learned all about human reproduction, yes, but I had not gone there for step-by-step instructions on how to make a baby. I was 13. I wanted to understand *sexuality*, not reproduction. Why had I been having such strange, new feelings? Was I becoming a man? What did that even mean?

In the months and years that followed, I turned to my buddies to discuss these and other important matters. Equally primitive in our understandings, we were like monkeys teaching monkeys about the finest arts. We told grossly exaggerated stories about our various romantic explorations, leaving out much of the truth—especially on our common mishaps as young lovers. The result: we never learned much from our

mishaps and were doomed to repeat them over and over again. We therefore spent much of young adulthood breaking hearts, our own included.
Together we became masters in the art of courting future ex-girlfriends.

It took more than a decade of bumbling around in the dark like this
to develop basic understandings about masculinity and sexuality. Long in
coming though they may have been, these understandings finally brought
about an emerging sense of self and, at long last, insights on both what it
meant to be a man and what it meant to be a lover.

Understandings nourish and empower your intelligence. They allow
you to act with mastery in your various pursuits, great or small. For
example, if you understand what a can opener is and how it functions,
a whole world of canned goods becomes available to you. Without this
understanding a can opener is just an odd looking object taking up space
in your kitchen, and canned nourishment is likely inaccessible to you.

Cruising about through daily experiences, your intelligence gathers
little bits of information such as images, sounds, smells, feelings, words,
phrases, and basic facts. Like bricks, these little bits of knowledge aren't
worth much on their own. By putting them together with one another
your intelligence builds them up into greater architectures of *understanding*. It uses these understandings to make sense of everything that goes on
within and around you. In doing so, it drives you along through life with
increasing power and success.

At the demand of an angry parent, a child may reluctantly agree to
repeat the words, "I promise to be more *respectful.*" These words are of
little value, however, if the child does not have a core understanding of
what they mean.

Take a moment to think about what *respect* really is. Explain it to
yourself.

You may notice that your understanding of respect is a very sophisticated construction of various other words and ideas, so much so that
perhaps you are not even sure where to begin to describe it. This understanding has been assembled over years, maybe even decades, through
countless thoughts and experiences. A young child's understanding of this
word is far less sophisticated than yours, as it has spent less time in development. When using this word with a child, you may think that the two
of you share the same understanding about it, but you do not. This word
means something much more basic to the child.

Intelligence continually adds to your understandings, building them up, keeping them in a constant state of evolution. Each time you come across a situation or piece of information that seems new, or that conflicts with understandings you already hold, your intelligence attempts to reconcile the new with the old. It synthesizes them into greater, more sophisticated understandings. Over the years layers upon layers of sophistication are added. Eventually, some of your understandings become so sophisticated and powerful that we give them a special name; we call them *wisdom*. Refined over decades, their power stands in a simple eloquence.

Understanding nourishes our brilliant state of intelligence. There are many kinds of understandings that we can work to develop—physical, intellectual, artistic, emotional, social, spiritual, and so on. Each nourishes a different aspect of our brilliance—the Babe Ruth within, or the Einstein, or the Dickinson, or the Hepburn, or the Shakespeare, or the Gandhi.

Three innate mechanisms allow us to build understanding. Used in conjunction with one another they fuel and empower the multifaceted brilliance available to each of us:

Exposure

Just as the digestive system absorbs nourishment for your body, so the senses absorb nourishment for your intelligence. By exposing yourself to a wide range of experiences, media, and materials, you feed your intelligence, nourishing its growth. Activities, studies, sports, hobbies, arts, jobs, travels, social and real-world experiences each flood your intelligence with unique forms of information, giving it loads of raw material to work with. Each new bit of information is a building block that can be used to construct increasingly sophisticated understandings about yourself and the world around you. Quite simply, exposure feeds the intelligence. Realize, however, that once exposed to something, the exposure cannot be undone. Once exposed to a dose of heroin, cocaine, or alcohol, for example, your intelligence never forgets the experience.

Reflection

Have you ever taken a class where much of your learning just scattered to the wind, never really taking hold in your mind? Exposure to information in-and-of itself does not build understanding. *Pondering* that information while it is fresh in your mind, thinking it over or talking about it with others—this is what allows you take that raw material and build with it. Reflection can take many forms, including note-taking, writing, using your imagination, making flow charts, engaging in artistic expressions, practicing physical movements, and so forth. Teaching something that you just learned about to someone else is a particularly powerful form, as is a good conversation or argument. Reflection is an extremely powerful tool for personal development of every kind. Various exercises in the previous chapter and in later chapters make use of it.

Application

Information is of little value unless you actually do something with it. The highest quality learning occurs when you apply your knowledge or understanding to a real-world purpose. It goes without saying that the information in this book is useless until you use it. Then, and only then, is its true power unleashed. By applying information that you have absorbed toward some purpose, using it to take action, you create a real-life context that gives the information unforgettable meaning. Consider the television addict's dilemma: while TV exposes you to information, yes, lounging there for hours on end keeps you from making quality use of that information. You watch other people have experiences; you watch *them* take action. For you, opportunity is lost.

Adults often tend to over-emphasize *exposure* when trying to support a child's intellectual development. They give too much information with too little emphasis on the child's personal *reflections* or *applications*. Because all three of these mechanisms are equally important when building understanding, this unbalanced approach yields a kind of intellectual malnourishment.

On the day of my fated meeting with Dr. Hill, I had walked into his office with thirteen years of exposure to information regarding sexuality, little of which made any sense to me. I had hoped to finally talk with someone about all those countless bits of information already floating around inside my head. I did not need more bits just yet. I needed to explore the questions lurking deep inside me with someone who could help me put the pieces together.

For example, why was I sprouting hair in strange places? Why wasn't I afraid of bullies anymore? Why did cute girls now scare me more than bullies ever had? Why did I stay after Ms. French's seventh period history class each day stamping the chalk out of her erasers and cleaning her chalkboard? Why was I getting the worst grade in her class when she was my favorite teacher? Why did I feel like a slave in her presence? Why did this slavery feel so good and so bad at the same time? Was something wrong with me?

Understanding is the foundation of success. With it comes the clarity to see things for what they are and thus the ability to act effectively in each of our everyday experiences.

Young children naturally use *exposure, reflection,* and *application* all day long in a balanced manner to build understandings, often through play. If and when adults take this balanced approach, much like young explorers uncovering great mysteries all around, we soon find our inherent brilliance nourished once again, and with it we experience a fresh fascination and enthusiasm for the human experience.

Awakening Your Own Brilliance

Have you ever noticed that intelligence seems to screech to a halt when someone is upset? He may lose the ability to listen well to others. She may get very quiet or very loud. They both say things they don't mean and do things they later regret. Emotional charge fills the air. Rationality and reason are suddenly nowhere to be found.

Human intelligence has two main modes of operation. *Brilliance* is the free-flowing state of your conscious intelligence. It acts quickly and creatively, directing your personal power to make keen use of information and opportunities at hand. *Reactivity*, by contrast, is a downshift to your mechanical, automatic mode of intelligence. All it can do is run old, patterned behaviors—generally in an attempt to cope with distress.

Brilliance allows you to approach situations as both an artist and scientist, masterfully making connections, solving problems, and expressing yourself. It uses ideas that you read or hear about like launch pads, rocketing off of them with fresh insights about life and love. It drives your actions with the prowess of an Olympic athlete, drawing the very best of yourself into everything you do. It is driven by your conscious intelligence.

Reactivity serves to keep you alive and kicking in times of overwhelm. It responds reflexively, like a youngster crying out in a tantrum. Reliant upon patterned behaviors that were developed during times of past distress—many in childhood—it causes you to behave immaturely, often in moments when maturity is what you need most. It is driven by your mechanical intelligence.

We tend to become increasingly *reactive* as we grow older. By the age of 13 we spend far less time—if any time at all—in our natural state of *brilliance*. This results from a long-term buildup of emotional charge in the intelligence and the inability to properly release this charge.

Each day we are confronted by things that we do not know or understand. We are called to use skills that we have not yet fully developed. We are forced to suppress natural instincts in order to behave in a civilized manner. We are required to cope with failure and uncertainty, insult and injury, adaptation and survival.

Distressed by these and other circumstances, our conscious intelligence is easily overwhelmed. It downshifts to its mechanical mode, *reacting* with patterned behaviors that were created under similar circumstances in the past, sometimes the very distant past. Though these reactions save us from total paralysis, they do not necessarily match the circumstances at hand very closely or effectively. The greater the mismatch, the more *irrational* the response is.

For example, a man who was forced to fend for himself as a child finds himself reactively pulling away from his wife in a moment when her support is crucial to his survival. As she tries to take the carpet cutter from his hand, he hollers, "leave me alone! I don't need a doctor! I can take care of this myself! I just have to get my damn wrist to stop spurting blood everywhere! All I need is another a towel!" Fifteen minutes later he is in critical condition, loaded onto an ambulance in great haste by paramedics.

Intelligence has the ability to release distress in order to regain its fully conscious state of brilliance. Laughter and tears are two common release mechanisms. You may actually feel the dissipation of energy while they are happening, and you are likely to enjoy a more awakened, radiant state of mind shortly thereafter.

In the bustle of our everyday lives it is often not safe or opportune to release distress. We therefore repress it in order to retain some degree of functionality, storing it as a kind of emotional charge in the intelligence.

Over time these charges accumulate. Whenever circumstances arise that resonate with old, stored emotional charges, those charges can be instantly reactivated. Intelligence automatically downshifts to its mechanical mode. The stored distress reawakens and with it, the behavior patterns developed during the original experience.

The more charges we accumulate, the more *reactive* we become. Our sights are clouded by a haze of unprocessed, hurt feelings. We find ourselves in frequent misunderstandings and must rely upon old, patterned behaviors to get us through them. We become encumbered by inhibitions, self-consciousness and fear. Over time these various manifestations of reactivity tend to build up within us, reducing us to an increasingly polluted and therefore "feeble mentality." Furthermore, they cause us to burn through personal power inefficiently and unproductively.

To clear this haze of emotional charge, and to reclaim the brilliance and power of a well maintained conscious intelligence, several common mechanisms are inherently available to us. Each helps us to manage distress and prevent us from being overwhelmed. All but one are effective. They are described as follows:

[1] TAKING PAUSE

In moments of emotional charge we are usually unable to rationally attend to matters at hand. We may say offensive things or act belligerently. By learning to recognize the presence of this charge we can train ourselves to take pause at these times—putting conversations on hold, saving decisions for later, and stepping away from expensive dishware. We can attend instead to managing our charge and thus quickly regain our radiant intelligence. Anger, anxiety, inflexibility, frustration, resistance, guilt, and sadness are all common indicators of emotional charge, each accompanied by distinctive energies and feelings. Learn to recognize them and you gain control over what to do with them.

[2] CONSCIOUS RELEASE

Many of us learned in childhood to repress our emotions, willing them into submission in order to remain semi-functional. More effective is to consciously relinquish this overwhelming energy, imagining its release from your body like sunlight out to distant planets. During the times when you identify a feeling of emotional charge inside, simply take a few deep breaths and relax your body. With each exhalation, imagine releasing your distress to a faraway place where it can be cleansed and refreshed. By using this *intentional breath*, you can regain composure fairly easily and with it, your conscious intelligence.

[3] EMOTIONAL RELEASE

Distress, charge, and energy overloads are powerfully released through emotion. Yawning releases tension. Trembling releases terror. Crying releases grief. Laughter releases embarrassment, awkwardness and fear. These mechanisms keep our energies flowing properly, breaking up the charges and blockages that disable us. Unfortunately, yawning and laughter are often seen as disrespectful, while crying and trembling are taken as signs of weakness. It might seem strange to imagine a time when people yawn, laugh, cry, or tremble openly. To evolved members of a future society, however, it will seem much stranger to imagine a time when people expended needless energy suppressing the natural mechanisms of intellectual health and recuperation.

[4] CREATING DRAMA

Though emotion is a powerful mechanism for managing charge, some people develop the habit of misusing it, recycling the same charge over and over again without ever releasing it. This tends to arise when someone gets something out of being emotional, like receiving attention, being cared for, or manipulating others. Before long we get addicted to our own distress. We find ourselves listening to the same sad songs over and over again, or whining to the same friends about the same problems, or getting into the same arguments with the same people. This addictive behavior is non-productive and self-defeating. It's best to simply *cut it out*.

[5] SHIFTING FOCUS

Where attention is directed, energy flows. Conscious intelligence can therefore be maintained by simply shifting attention away from distress. By focusing instead on any one of the extraordinary wonders that surround us, we halt ourselves from feeding our hurt and charge. A choice always exists—to wallow in distress, polluting ourselves and the world around us, or to turn our attention toward that which is positive and productive. Exercise, hobbies, and various outlet activities are powerful mechanisms for directing attention off of distress, if not overused.

[6] OFFERING COMPASSION

The easiest way to manage emotional charge is to avoid taking on the charge of others. We often pass hurts around like hot-potatoes—husband to wife, parent to child, friend to friend, and so on. Inflicting hurt on others is a feeble and desperate effort to release charge. The antidote is *compassion*, which halts the infection of hurt that might otherwise spread through our families, communities and societies. By recognizing when those among us are emotionally charged, then making the choice not to take their emotional charge personally or reactively, but rather, *compassionately*, we become immune to their charges. Maintaining composure and clarity, simply offering quiet and caring attention to those who are charged, we support the release of their old, festering hurts. By offering our compassion in this manner, we serve to clear the atmosphere for us all.

Consider the case of Mitchell, age twelve. I was brought in to teach his sixth grade class after four other teachers had been driven away, a situation attributed largely to Mitchell's antics. I was told that Mitchell was an incorrigible child, that I'd better have my wits about me.

During my first conversation with the class, Mitchell halted my introduction by offering a haunting imitation of President George W. Bush. He informed his fellow Americans that *teacherism* would not be tolerated, and that evil-doers would be banished. I laughed along with the other students, truly impressed by his improvisational skills, then proceeded with my introduction.

That afternoon, I invited Mitchell to skip algebra period so that he and I could hang out for a little while. We sat down at a table together.

"How do you like school?" I asked casually.

"It sucks," he replied.

I smiled, appreciating his candor.

Noticing my reaction, he gazed curiously at me. "What?" he said.

"Who would guess that you of all people think that school sucks. You seem to be having such a great time."

A mischievous glint appeared in the corner of his eye.

"Tell me about it," I said, encouraging him to reflect. "Why don't you like school?"

"Why?" He studied me for a moment, then leaned against the table. "Because teachers hate me," he said. "You're gonna hate me too." He whipped the long bangs of hair away from his eyes with the shake of his head. "That's just how it goes, I guess."

I smiled again. "Such certainty," I said.

"You don't know what it's like," he retorted. "Having to be me all day. Having everyone always *at* me, always trying to turn me into something I don't want to be. Especially you teacher guys. You're the worst."

Fascinated, I sat there quietly, eagerly awaiting more.

"Last year at my old school I had Mr. Trumble," he said, with an almost violent emphasis on *Trumble*. "Mr. Trumble had this whistle, right? He'd stand next to me with it, and each time I'd start to talk he'd blow that damn thing right in my ear." Mitchell's tone was sharp. It felt like a high voltage had suddenly charged the air.

"Keep going," I said.

"This one time …" He swallowed awkwardly, as if embarrassed by the mere memory. "This one time, Trumble whistled at me so loud that my ear started ringing real bad. It just kept ringing and ringing. It totally freaked me out, but I couldn't tell anyone, right? Because I was the one who was gonna get in trouble. I'm always the one. Idiot!"

"I'm starting to see why you don't like school," I said. "It's too bad, though. I don't often have the opportunity to work with someone as powerful as you."

Mitchell glared at me.

"I'm serious," I said. "You're funny. Witty. Honest as they come. A natural leader." I leaned against the table in a position similar to his. "What's holding you back, Mitch? What do you need?"

He stared at me like a deer in headlights, his eyes growing wet and glassy.

"Right," I said. "Maybe that's what you need. Why not be powerful about it?"

A tear spilled from his eye and rolled down his cheek.

"It's okay," I said. "Let it go."

Lowering his head to the table, he began to cry. He wrapped his arms tightly around his face. "I hate myself," he said, his voice muddled with emotion.

I felt the impulse to say something, but didn't want to interrupt his process. Instead, I just sat with him, offering my undivided attention.

He looked up at me from time to time as if to check that I was still there. When our eyes met he'd break into another deep sob, more and more like a young child each time.

After about ten minutes the emotion seemed to subside.

Mitchell peered up at me, and this time that mischievous glint had returned to his eyes. I tried to over-dramatically return the look, manufacturing a goofy, mischievous glint of my own. He chuckled, rolling his eyes. I chuckled too, a little embarrassed by my own antics. The laughter was strangely contagious, and soon we were both in stitches.

After a little while, we headed back to class in silence. Just outside the door, Mitchell stopped me. "Hey," he said. "Check this out. I just figured something out."

"Oh yeah? What's that?"

"Anger's like the flu," he said, beaming with pride.

I gazed curiously at him. "What do you mean?" I asked.

"You can catch it from other people," he said.

I nodded, mulling it over. "Brilliant," I said. "You gotta write that one down. And while you're at it, think about this. *When you learn not to take other people's emotional crud personally—*" I dramatically cleared my throat. "*Then you become immune.*" I winked at him.

He smiled, thinking it over. "Right," he said. He slugged me fondly in the shoulder. "You gotta teach me how to do that."

In the weeks that followed, Mitchell rallied the troops to make up for months of lost learning, reinventing himself all the while. With his help, we managed to cover nearly a year's worth of material in just under four months. During that time, Mitchell climbed from being one of the lowest performing students in class to our second highest achiever.

A single, compassionate encounter with a fellow human being allowed Mitchell to bring about some much needed emotional cleansing, after which he was able to enthusiastically apply himself to nourishing his own intelligence, and even helping others to do the same.

In this manner, the release of charge is essential to intellectual health. With it, our energies begin to flow properly once again, and we find access to the radiance and power of our innate state of brilliance.

Chapter 2 Exercises

Exercise 2a: Active Reflection

Active reflection is a supremely powerful technique for supporting personal growth. It can be used to improve a relationship, enhance performance at work, advance a skill or talent, sharpen an understanding, make the most of a success or failure, or support a need such as carving out more personal time. Whether we realize it or not, we each use this technique all day long. The more deliberate we are about using it, however, the more powerful its results are. The following four "active reflection" steps can be used personally or in partnership with other people:

Step 1: Analysis

Choose something that you wish to develop. For example, pick a technique on pages 33-35 that seems valuable. What do you understand about the purpose or value of the technique? Read the material several times, trying to better understand it with each pass. What about it is noteworthy? Think the matter through.

Step 2: Context

Now consider the matter in a specific context. For example, read through the story on page 35 and look for evidence of your chosen technique in action. Think about people you know or book/movie scenes that display the matter in action. Consider various experiences in your own life where it might have been of value. Apply your understanding to different real world contexts, further thinking it through.

Step 3: Imagination

Think of a related scenario in your real, everyday life. Imagine playing out whatever it is that you are trying to develop within this scenario. Create your own mental movie of what solid success might look like. If you are working on a technique or skill, *see* yourself as a master. If you are reflecting on a talent, such as your golf swing, *imagine* making a perfect stroke over and over again. Imagination is a surprisingly powerful mode of practice, valuable in any endeavor.

Step 4: Action

Set an intention to do something that specifically relates to the matter you are reflecting on. Give yourself an assignment. For example, consider a situation that you know is likely to come up in the next few days, one where you can apply the skills or understandings that you are developing. Think of what you will need to set yourself up for success. Then go for it! Whether you succeed or fail, the experience will be of value so long as you follow it up with a new round of reflection the following evening or morning. As you engage in this later round of reflection, think about what you might do differently next time.

Active reflection helps you to truly absorb and internalize a learning experience, allowing you to avoid repeating it over and over again. The more frequently you reflect on any particular matter, the quicker and more effectively you develop *mastery*. The overall process need not take a long time. You can think through it while walking or hiking, on your commute to work or school, or lying in bed before sleep. If you partner up with somebody and dialogue about it, the process is even more powerful.

Exercise 2b: Developing Emotional Clarity

At times of distress, conscious intelligence is overwhelmed. Under such circumstances, two things tend to happen: (1) we attempt to emote the distress, and (2) we react with patterned behaviors.

The problem with *reactivity* is that we rarely notice it happening. Intelligence downshifts to its mechanical mode. Little if any conscious intelligence remains. As a result, we are generally unable to effectively solve problems or engage in rational communication.

It is possible to train ourselves to increase conscious function at these times. This is an important step toward managing our charge, and toward regaining and then maintaining our intellectual brilliance.

To begin, read this chapter on "The Art of Brilliance" once again to deepen your understanding of it. As you do, make a list of the common emotional charges and reactions that commonly come up for you. *Do you get angry? What happens when you do? Do you get sad? How do you behave when feeling that way?*

Create a chart with four columns across the top. Label them as follows: "The Issue," "Circumstances," "Emotional Charge," and "Reaction." Input your common charges into this chart. Figure 1 offers an example of how to input the information.

In the first column, briefly describe the basic issue that arises for you. In the second column, note the circumstances under which each issue arises. In the third column, note the feelings associated with each issue such as sadness, anger, apprehension, fear, embarrassment, shame, tension, and so on. In the fourth column, note your common behavior patterns for each of these specific issues or charges. Common examples include pouting, violence, withdrawal, paralysis, eye rolling, judgment, and belligerence.

As you fill in this chart, be honest with yourself. If you don't allow yourself to see your charges and reactions, it is very hard to overcome them. If you don't overcome them, you may resign yourself to relinquishing your inherent brilliance to them.

Once you have your chart, the next step is to set an intention: "I will notice when charge arises inside me—during the actual moment when it arises." At this point in the assignment, you don't have to do anything about the charge if it does arise. Try not to judge it one way or another. Just notice it while it's happening. Gather more information about what triggers it, or how it feels, or how it causes you to behave. Reflect for five minutes each night or morning on the previous 24 hours. *Do you remember any other moment when you became emotionally charged? Were you able to recognize it at the time? What were the major indicators that charge was present?* Add new discoveries to your chart.

If you find that you were unable to notice emotional charge in the moment that it was active, don't worry about it. Recognizing it after the fact is still valuable. It will prepare you to notice it more clearly during future occurrences.

With time and persistence this exercise will significantly raise your conscious awareness of charge and reactivity. You will begin to separate the *content of an issue* from the *emotional charge* that is triggered. Your next step is to develop the technique of "pause" discussed on page 33. This will give you more conscious control over how you choose to react or behave under such circumstances. The previous "Active Reflection" technique can help you to accomplish this goal fairly quickly.

Once you train yourself to take pause in moments of charge, you are then ready to explore the various techniques for releasing or managing charge listed on pages 33-35. This will allow you to truly reverse your reactivity and revitalize that brilliant state of intelligence with which you were born.

The Issue	Circumstances	Emotional Charge	Reaction
Not being perfect	Thinking back on something stupid I said at work	Embarrassment; shame	Beating up on myself in my mind; physically wincing at the thought of it
My child's poor manners at an important dinner affair	Trudy picked up her steak with her fingers to eat it, which reflected poorly on me.	Embarrassment; shame	Withdrawing from conversation; seething inside
Judgment	Showing up to a party overdressed	Apprehension; awkwardness	Trying to avoid being visible; cautiousness
Feeling unloved	Trudy telling me she hates me during a temper tantrum	Sadness	Withdrawing
Feeling Misunderstood	Being reprimanded for my handling of a difficult situation at work; not being able to explain how it was best under the circumstances	Frustration; anger; embarrassment; shame	Shutting down; not speaking up for myself
Double standards	Generally getting attacked for things by people who do the same things themselves	Frustration; resentment	Getting defensive; striking back, and then feeling like a jerk
Expectation	Sara showing up 45 minutes late	Frustration	Withdrawing; being a jerk
Feeling responsible for other people's issues	Wanting to make Larry feel better about getting fired	Tension; awkwardness	Lying to Larry about his poor performance, trying to help him feel better
Feeling unappreciated	The kids whining and complaining about a family trip that I put together thinking that they'd love it	Frustration; anger; resentment; embarrassment	Being a jerk; lying by saying that this is our last family trip ever

FIGURE 1. *Example of creating an "Inventory of Emotional Charges"*

Essential Questions

Take a few moments to ponder the following questions. Allow yourself to come up with at least three answers to each question as a means of self-discovery. Keep a written record of your answers in a log or journal.

- Who or what has had the greatest influence in guiding the course of my life up until today?

- From this moment forward, what changes would I like to make regarding who or what guides the course of my life?

- What are my three most important questions in life, and how do they influence my actions?

CHAPTER 3

The Art of Focus

*An elder Cherokee chief took his grandchildren into the forest
and sat them down. He said to them, "a fight is going on inside
me. This is a terrible fight, a fight between two wolves. One wolf
is the wolf of fear, anger, arrogance and greed. The other wolf is
the wolf of courage, kindness, humility and love."*

*The children were very quiet, listening to their grandfather
with both their ears.*

*He then said to them, "this same fight between the two wolves
that is going on inside of me, it is going on inside of you, and
inside every person."*

*The children thought about it for a minute. Then one of them
asked, "Grandfather, which wolf will win the fight?"*

The chief said quietly, "the one you feed."

—CHEROKEE FOLKLORE

Growth of any kind requires energy. It requires large amounts of energy.
In the plant kingdom, the sun has tremendous power in directing the
growth of its subjects—the various plant species—because it is their primary source of energy. It is their food. The angles of their leaves, the
development of their branches, even the orientations of their crowning
sprouts, are all influenced by the position of the sun as it crosses the sky.

Unlike plants, we human beings carry within us an energy source that
can be used to direct our own growth. Much like using a precision flash-
light, we can focus this energy in a narrow beam upon specific qualities, or
can shine it in a wide spread upon many things at once. We can use it to
influence the growth of those around us, or to sprout and grow whatever
we desire within ourselves.

This inner sunlight is most commonly known as *attention*. It is a stream of personal power that continually flows through our consciousness. The single most important talent in the art of personal development is that of harnessing, focusing, and employing attention.

Imagine a scientist who conducts research deep inside a cave. He has a fertile plot of soil, seeds for many crops, plenty of water, and a full-spectrum growth lamp. He sets his lamp to shine outward in a wide spread across his underground garden and sprouts a large assortment of crops. It takes a while for these crops to mature, however, as the power of his lamp is spread thin. He narrows the focus of the beam onto a smaller section of the garden, harnessing a greater intensity of light. The crops spotlighted by the beam begin to flourish, while those in the dim light beyond begin to wither.

A similar experiment can be conducted using human attention as the energy source, shining it upon human behaviors, characteristics, or objectives. This experiment yields similar results. *The things we focus attention on tend to grow; the things we ignore tend to wither, or must seek other energy sources for growth.*

If we focus with high intensity on a specific goal, we can powerfully accomplish that goal in short order. If we broaden our attention to encompass a wider spread of goals, the pace of accomplishment slows because each individual goal has less energy feeding it.

Those who do not learn to focus their attention tend to have little control over what grows in their lives. The most powerful people we encounter do not necessarily have more intrinsic power than anyone else. They have often simply developed mastery over their attention; thus they know how to focus what power they do have with great efficiency.

A baseball coach repeats the same phrase to his young batters at least twenty times a practice and forty times a game. What is that phrase?

"Keep your eye on the ball." Coach recognizes that where attention is focused, power is directed. The more mastery a young batter has over her attention, the more control she has in directing her power.

Musician and teacher Robert Fripp once said, "According to *USA Today*, the average length of an attention span of a man in America is 23 minutes. Above that, more mature adults can hold their attention on something for 45 minutes, whether they like it or not. Above that requires training."

To powerfully affect your ongoing development, you must command your own attention. In this pursuit, three topics are of value:

1. **The Nature of Attention**—Recognizing what attention is and how it functions.

2. **Clear and Lucid Awareness**—Learning to increase conscious control of your attention.

3. **The Power of Focused Attention**—Developing the discipline to harness the immense attention available to you.

The Nature of Attention

Attention nurtures the growth of that upon which it shines. If you focus attention on your weaknesses, continually shining light upon the ways in which you are lacking, you tend to grow disappointed in yourself. This focus of energy on incompetence leaves less energy for competence. Thus your actions become sloppier, weaker, lacking in vital energy.

If instead you focus attention on the strengths you wish to develop, this energy leads you to engage in strengthening activities, applying your power directly and efficiently toward your growth. You see yourself growing and begin to feel stronger and more capable.

To effectively wield attention, it helps to have a thorough understanding of how it functions. The following key qualities of attention are important to recognize:

- Attention can be used to influence the growth of any human being, including one's self and others.

- Attention does not discriminate in what it grows. Just as vegetables and weeds thrive under the same sunlight, by focusing your attention on that which is best in someone, you grow it. By focusing your attention on that which is worst in someone, you grow that.

- Similar streams of attention combine to amplify one another. Opposing streams cancel each other out. If one person applies *encouraging* attention where another applies *discouragement*, the stream with stronger intensity or focus tends to overcome the weaker.

- Whereas sunlight is a pure form of energy, attention is impure. It carries with it the thoughts and feelings of the person who is shining it, just as the light from a movie projector carries with it the images of the film through which it shines.

Because attention directs your energy, how and where you focus your attention determines how and where your energy is applied. In parenting, we sometimes come to focus attention on just a few of our children's attributes or behaviors, spotlighting those few with greater energy than all the others combined. This tendency is particularly common with attributes or behaviors that we find challenging or similar to our own weaknesses.

Unfortunately, attention does not discriminate in what it grows. By focusing on our children's difficult or negative attributes and behaviors, the energy of our attention causes them to grow or even thrive.

Take for example the case of a frustrated single parent. Michael has two children, a boy and a girl. Sarah, the oldest, is like most children; she is a package of boundless love, playfulness, imagination, dynamic energy, unique likes and dislikes, quirky mannerisms, strengths and weaknesses—all rolled into one.

In the midst of her parents' messy divorce Sarah falls into a slump, missing her mom terribly. Michael explains that mommy moved away without telling him where and that there's nothing he can do about it.

Uninterested in the facts, feeling unacknowledged for her pain, Sarah begins to act out her anguish. She refuses to take baths, to get dressed for school, or to go to sleep unless daddy "does it the way mommy used to do it."

Going through some grief of his own, Michael is hurt by Sarah's behavior and finds himself frustrated by her "selfishness" and "defiance." His attention begins to target these two qualities, focusing energy upon them with his rising frustration. He forgets about the big picture—that Sarah is alive and breathing, blood pumping through her adorable being to nourish her smiles, tears, and tantrums alike. Despite this miracle of life radiating before him, all Michael can see is a selfish brat.

As the focus of his attention narrows upon Sarah's selfish and defiant behaviors, like sunlight, this attention begins to grow and perpetuate those behaviors. After all, Sarah is aware of what daddy sees in her and, whether his assessment is accurate or not, she is filled with the energy of his opinion. She soon begins to identify herself as a selfish brat and acts accordingly.

At any moment Michael can change his mind about Sarah. He can step back and look at the big picture of who she is—that young, living, breathing human being with joys and sorrows. He can simply listen to and acknowledge Sarah's grief without taking it personally or without trying to fix it. He can redirect his attention to Sarah's many strengths and, in doing so, grow an entirely different set of behaviors in a single afternoon.

One day after school, Michael decides to change his approach with Sarah. He sets out to make loving and attentive observations about her. In a brief exchange, he intentionally redirects the focus of his attention and immediately ends their power struggle.

"Look at the way you snuggle your little brother," he says warmly. "You sure are a caring big sister. We're so lucky to have you in our lives." He gives her a big hug and kiss. "Do you want to play with Timmy while I get dinner ready? Or maybe we could all make dinner together? What do you think would be best?"

Human attention is a highly sophisticated mechanism, much like a movie projector. Its light shines through the film of your beliefs, emotions and ideas about things, projecting them out onto the objects you see. Those objects, especially people, serve as your movie screens. They reflect the things you project upon them with an uncanny realness.

In this manner, you turn the things you look at into the subjects of your own ideas about them. This is partly why one's view of reality is said to be *subjective* rather than *objective*. The world becomes the *subject* of your own ideas about it, the reflecting screen.

When dad identifies Sarah as *selfish* and *defiant*, he projects this idea upon her. As a result he quickly and easily notices her subtlest acts of defiance or even imagines them where they do not exist. All the while, he misses the obvious, caring things that Sarah does for the family because he is so focused on her "selfishness."

Like a pocket knife whittling down a piece of driftwood into a small sculpture, what we choose to notice and what we choose to ignore whittle down the very thing we are looking at, conforming it to our beliefs and ideas about it.

This allows us to use other people as materials for our own education. We project our own weaknesses, judgments, self-doubts, and emotions upon them. We whittle away many of their shining strengths and gifts until much of what we see is but a caricature of the actual person there before us. We then try to help this person correct these weaknesses, which helps us to correct them in ourselves.

Unfortunately, the sunlight of human attention is so powerful that it can actually grow the qualities of our projections in the very people upon whom we are projecting, causing them to conform to our ideas about them. Thus we sometimes create the very problems in our counterparts that we are trying to fix in ourselves.

I recently spoke with the mother of one of my students from years past. I commented that her daughter was a truly remarkable young woman.

Gina laughed—an exuberant, snorty kind of laugh. "Remember when Sheila was in your class?" she asked. "How weird she was?"

Sheila had gone through a bit of an identity struggle at the time, but I hadn't thought of her as weird. "What do you mean?" I asked.

"I just … I wanted her to be normal," Gina confessed. "You know how it is. Torture. You want your kid to be great. Or at least normal." She shook her head as if trying to shake off an old anguish. "She and I fought all the time. Over her hair. Her friends. Her drawings. That stupid stuffed animal."

I thought back to the conflicts Sheila got into over her little stuffed teddy-bear. She was its champion, its protector. She wouldn't let anyone speak badly of it.

"A year ago I gave up the fight," Gina said abruptly. "I couldn't change her, no matter how I tried. *She is who she is*, I decided, and let it go at that. I even made myself tell her that I loved her just the way she was, even if it was only a little bit true."

She chuckled to herself. "Scott," she said, and then took my hand as if to emphasize a point. "I swear this is how it happened. We stopped fighting that day. It was like suddenly waking up from a bad dream. I look at her now and can't even believe it. She's amazing. Was she always like this? I can't honestly say."

Clear and Lucid Awareness

All day and night long, you take information in through your senses, and then interpret that information. Lucidity is the accuracy of your interpretation, the measure of your mental clarity. The higher your lucidity, the greater your ability to *perceive*—to make sense of things that go on within and around you.

If in the presence of you and others, a man yells angrily and belligerently, is this because he is mad at you, or because he is mad at someone or something else, or because he is simply mad? One of these perceptions is more accurate than the others, and each may very well trigger a different response in you. The more accurate your perception, the more effective your response.

Your mind is a primary resource in the ongoing creation of your being. The more lucid it is, the more effective and powerful its art becomes. It has both conscious and subconscious regions that operate independently of one another. The conscious region works within your awareness, while the subconscious region works without your awareness. This strange partnership has a tendency to muddle up your lucidity.

Much like a projectionist in a movie theater, your subconsciousness operates behind the scenes. Hidden away in the projection room of your mind, it secretly loads films onto the projector of your awareness, adding your underlying beliefs, emotions, and ideas to the light of your attention, and therefore to everything you see. By loading inaccurate or outdated films, your subconsciousness lowers your lucidity.

For example, in sleep one's lucidity is generally quite low. We are unaware that our bodies are asleep or that we are dreaming. Our regular, waking consciousness is seated in the theater of the mind, drowsy and passive. The subconscious projectionist—a true night owl—seizes the opportunity to play all its favorite movies, one after another. These movies (our dreams) add tremendous amounts of fictional information to what we are perceiving. The consciousness reacts as if this information is real, as if the people and forces projected on the screen are actually acting upon us.

One night while asleep, having had too much to drink before bed, your bladder begins to balloon beyond capacity. In your dream, feeling socked in the stomach, you run through the cobblestone streets of a small town— fountains and waterfalls everywhere—believing that you are fleeing a Mafia goon who just slugged you below the belt for some reason that is not clear. Your subconsciousness has loaded a film, adding all sorts of fictional information to the perception of a full bladder. Rather than simply waking up to go urinate, your attention is diverted to playing out your fears and fantasies in a high-budget Hollywood gangster film.

With some effort, lucidity in sleep can be increased. You can learn to fully awaken the consciousness while your body remains asleep. You can take over the projector and direct everything that happens in the dream. You can remove the films altogether, turn the dream off, and simply experience the body asleep with full clarity. You can become aware of physical conditions around you, hearing nearby conversations or feeling temperature changes. You can awaken your body at will. An Internet search on the keywords "lucid dreaming" will turn up countless resources for developing this ability.

Right now as your consciousness is reading these words, your subconsciousness is simultaneously loading films onto the projector of your awareness. Though your lucidity is higher than when you dream, it is nowhere close to the top of its scale. Just as you can increase your lucidity level during sleep, you can increase it in the waking hours as well.

The more lucid you are, the more effectively your choices and behaviors serve you, because they match more closely the reality of goings-on inside and around you. The more lucid you become, the greater your control over your attention and thus the greater your control in who you become each and every moment.

There are several common qualities that lower one's lucidity:

- **Fear** Our fears tend to inhibit us from looking at, experiencing, and understanding the things that we are afraid of. For example, a fear of water keeps your feet firmly planted on dry land. The ocean therefore remains mysterious and frightening. An entire world exists just below the surface there, a world that your fear will not allow you to discover.

- **Self-Centeredness** As young children we are only aware of one point of view. Everyone and everything revolve around *me*. By simply putting his hands over his eyes a toddler can make the whole world disappear. With maturity comes the realization that all those other people out there have viewpoints of their own; the world continues to exist for them whether our eyes are opened or closed. As you emphasize the question of *What's in it for me?* you hold your hand over your eyes, blinding yourself to possibilities that exist beyond that tiny corner of the universe known as *mine*.

- **Closed-Mindedness** Chapter 2 on the Art of Brilliance explored the manner in which we develop understandings about the nature of everything within and around us. Our understandings continually evolve with each new experience, each new bit of information gathered. As we grow older we sometimes grow inflexible, rigidly holding to our core understandings as if they are finished, as if there is nothing new to learn or know. We then meet another barrier beyond which we are unable to see, the barrier of our own ignorance.

- **Neediness** When we are overly dependent upon others to fulfill our wishes and needs, much of our energy becomes dedicated toward manipulating those people to serve us. Less time and energy are available for developing our own skills, abilities, and talents. Yearning for the attention of others, we fool ourselves into believing that the most powerful tool of personal development exists outside ourselves, beyond our grasp. *I need attention!* But whose attention is it that you truly need?

The barriers that we run into throughout our lives—many of which are seemingly invisible and mysterious—result from circumstances right here before our very eyes, circumstances that we are simply unable to see. In many cases it's just a matter of taking our hands away from our eyes. By working to raise our lucidity, our barriers become increasingly visible. Once they are in plain view we can then work to overcome them.

The process by which we learn and develop ourselves is known as *education*. It does not end after seventh period or the day we graduate. It happens every moment of our lives, awake and asleep. The more active we are as students in this classroom of life, the more persistently we raise our lucidity.

As an interesting side benefit, our own increasing lucidity tends to catalyze the same lucidity in others around us. We raise the bar for everyone in our circle and in doing so, increase the potential of what we can become and achieve together. All of the exercises in this book support you in increasing your lucidity.

The Power of Focused Attention

The more you learn to focus your attention, the less you require the attention of others when trying to fulfill your own needs and ambitions.

You may have noticed that highly focused children tend to be rather self-sufficient and often have an energizing influence on others. You may also have noticed that scattered and unruly children tend to be quite needy and have a draining effect on others.

How often do we hear the frustrated parent say: "He's just doing that to get attention." This statement conveys a powerful truth, yet it is generally used to discount the very truth it is conveying. If a plant could ask for sunlight when it needed it, would we discount it for doing so?

Needy children and adults alike tend to yearn for attention, but it is not necessarily the attention of others for which they yearn. Ultimately it is *the discipline to focus their own attention* that they crave most, looking to everyone around them for help—especially those people whom they identify as *focused*.

Writer and comedian Dennis Miller once said, "There's no doubt about it; show business lures the people who didn't get enough love, attention, or approval early in life and have grown up to become bottomless, gaping vessels of terrifying, abject need. Please laugh."

It goes without saying that a parent's attention is essential to our development in early youth. Not only is it used to influence our growth; it is used to help us focus our own attention. *Mommy, watch me do this! Watch me do it again! Watch me again! And again!* As young children, we are generally unable to focus our own attention for sustained periods. Mom and dad lend us their attention, helping us to persist with our various activities. By directing focused attention upon us they help us to focus our own attention.

The highest quality attention available is that which is offered without conditions, hidden agendas, or expectations. Many adults were never given this kind of clean attention. They never learned to develop it and therefore cannot offer it to their children.

Fortunately, regardless of how much quality attention we receive from our parents, family members, and friends, there are eight powerful techniques that enable us to develop a clean focus of attention at any point in our lives:

[1] STUDYING

It is in our nature to learn. We do so constantly, whether we mean to or not. By *intentionally* setting out to study something or to develop various skills, abilities, and talents, we automatically harness our attention. Like a firefighter directing a stream of water into a burning building, we hold our attention in sharp focus as we apply it through sustained effort at a specific target.

[2] OBSERVING

We are surrounded by fellow community members who have developed finely tuned control over their attention. This includes artists, musicians, actors, dancers, athletes, orators, gardeners, construction workers, machinists, crafts-persons, and so on. By observing their talents live and in person, and tracking their focused use of attention, we vicariously discipline that same focus of attention within ourselves.

[3] QUESTIONING

The average four-year-old asks more than 400 questions a day. In the process, the child's intellect, lucidity, and focus develop at a remarkable pace. By asking thoughtful questions, we temporarily stop projecting our own thoughts and ideas all over the place and allow ourselves to gaze directly into the vast unknown. Spending more time with questions and less time with answers, we manage to increase our lucidity while flexing our focus at the same time.

[4] LISTENING

Our minds tend to run nonstop. When we are not talking to others, we talk to ourselves through an ongoing, internal dialogue. Even while listening to others this internal dialogue makes judgments, develops responses, sets agendas, and thinks ahead to what's next. By contrast, when we redirect ourselves to listen attentively without all the noise, we not only develop focus, but allow ourselves to truly take in other points of view, to see things from new perspectives.

[5] MEDITATING

To take "listening" one step further, we can quiet our thoughts even when no one else is talking. By allowing ourselves to be silent within we—like the movie screen—allow the world to project itself upon us for a change. While doing this we gain access to intuitive information and wisdom otherwise lost in the din of mental chatter.

[6] RISK-TAKING

Under the right circumstances our fear can catalyze us into a state of heightened attentiveness. By taking *reasonable* risks, putting ourselves in a controlled state of fear, we intentionally bump ourselves into heightened awareness. It is as if the ability to focus emerges out of thin air. In doing the very things we are afraid of we not only conquer our fears; we seize powerful control of our attention.

[7] TAKING ACTION

We have a wealth of energy that must be spent each day. Applying ourselves to physical activities, creative projects, labor, leadership, and other endeavors, we take the opportunity to harness attention in a manner that yields tangible results.

[8] BEING OF SERVICE

Few pursuits are as rewarding as giving to those in need. Such efforts are appreciated by more than just the people we serve. Other kindhearted folks and philanthropists rally around us to appreciatively channel their attention through our altruistic pursuits. We soon find ourselves commanding a greater supply of attention and have the opportunity to exercise focus over this potent, collective energy.

Attention is a resource as abundant as sunlight. It streams outward all day long whether we choose to tap into it or not. By developing conscious focus of our attention, we learn to harness one of the greatest creative powers available to humankind, one that happens to be freely available within ourselves at all times.

Once focused, the question then becomes: Where might we best choose to direct this power?

Chapter 3 Exercises

Exercise 3a: Using *Attention* to Develop an Attribute or Quality

Attention nourishes the growth of that upon which it shines. Unfortunately for many of us, our attention often flitters about. We don't really take the time to think about where we wish to focus it or what we wish to grow in our lives. As a result, we feed many unintentional or undesirable qualities in ourselves and others, and have difficulty developing the things that we most aspire to hold. This exercise will help you gain conscious command over the things that you are growing in yourself and others:

STEP 1: SELF-AWARENESS

What are the qualities, behaviors or attributes that you notice most regularly about yourself? List them. Does your list identify the ones that you most wish to nourish in yourself? Cross out those that you do not wish to perpetuate. Add new ones that you hope to develop in the coming years.

STEP 2: CREATING AN "INTENTION" PAGE

At the top of a separate page headed "Intention" write the words "I am … " followed by the one aspect of yourself that you most wish to develop. Choose only one. Beneath this statement list several reasons why this aspect is important to you (see Figure 2).

Now divide the bottom half of the page into two boxes and title them: (1) "Where or how I will look for *evidence* of my chosen personal aspect each day" and (2) "How I will *appreciate* the evidence that I find." In the first box, list thoughts or activities that you might engage in to develop your chosen attribute, or where you might find evidence of it in the things you already do. In the second box, list ways that you might allow yourself to appreciate this aspect in yourself when you find evidence of it. These are powerful techniques for focusing attention on whatever it is that you wish to develop in yourself. Optional: draw a sapling as depicted in Figure 2 to represent your chosen aspect, and draw the sun emitting small shafts of light to represent the focus of your attention.

Intention: I am Adventurous!

It is important for me to try new things, push my limits, expand my horizons, and to find excitement in even the most mundane experiences ...

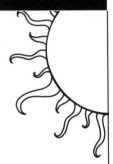

Where or how I will look for evidence of my chosen personal aspect each day:	How I will appreciate the evidence that I find:
• In seeking new opportunities • Approaching common situations in uncommon ways • Introducing myself to people I find interesting or engaging • Setting out to do one new thing each day • Trying new foods • Trying to see things from different points of view • Attempting something I don't think I'm capable of • Looking for ways to be fascinated during boring moments or situations	• Imagine the sunshine of my attention shining down on the sapling of my goal • Imagine that sapling basking in the sun, soaking it in, beginning to thrive • Taking a deep breath of happiness and enjoying the moment • Mentally patting myself on the back • Feeling the awe of an adventurer who just discovered something incredible • Imagine myself doing a goofy dance • Actually doing a goofy dance wherever I am • Crying out: "whoo-who!"

FIGURE 2. *Example of Creating an "Intention" Page*

STEP 3: FOCUS

For one day, try to think frequently about the aspect of yourself that you chose to develop. Look for evidence of it in your thoughts and actions, no matter how slight the evidence is. When *you do* recognize it, *take 15 seconds to appreciate it.* Imagine your *attention* nourishing this quality in you, shining upon it like sunlight, drawing it out. If at certain moments your attention begins to focus on some of the qualities or attributes that you crossed off your list, refocus yourself on the quality that you wish to develop.

STEP 4: REFLECTION

Before going to sleep, take five minutes to think back over your day. Ponder the following questions without judging yourself one way or another: *How much attention was I able to focus on my desired quality, even if in brief spurts? How often did my focus shift to undesired qualities? Was I able to redirect my attention? Did I take any actions to develop my desired quality beyond simply paying attention to it? Most importantly: what will I do differently tomorrow?* This reflection focuses attention on your desired growth, nourishing your progress each day. If you find evidence of growth, add to the drawing of the sapling as if it is growing into a tree. If you don't find evidence, add bigger shafts of sunlight to represent an increase in the focus of your attention. This use of art and imagination can have a powerful effect on improving your results the next day. Hold the image of sun and sapling in your mind.

Repeat steps 3 and 4 each day for a week or so. The more energy you put into them, the more you will get out of them. With solid effort, you will notice tangible growth over time and find yourself thinking about and doing things that promote the growth you seek.

Once you become comfortable with this technique, you can follow these same four steps to nourish a quality or attribute in someone else. If you choose to do so, step three is particularly important. *Look for evidence* of the quality that you are nourishing; *offer genuine appreciation* of this quality when you notice it.

Using this technique on someone else can sometimes feel manipulative. Realize that you influence others in this manner all the time, simply with less lucidity or awareness in the matter. This technique does not cause you to be more manipulative, but rather more thoughtful in how you inevitably influence others through the natural course of each day.

Exercise 3b: Sharpening the Focus of Your Attention

Attention is the energy source that drives all of your conscious activities and nourishes your growth. The greater your ability to focus attention, the more power you have over how your life unfolds.

Begin this exercise by rereading "The Power of Focused Attention" on page 52. This will help to deepen your understanding before you proceed with the exercise. Pay special attention to the "focus" techniques listed on pages 53-54. As you read through them, consider the one technique that stands out for you. Perhaps you recognize it as an area of weakness, or an area of interest, or something that you've thought about developing at times in the past. It doesn't matter which technique you choose. Any one of them can help you become more aware and attentive within a week.

Use the following steps to develop your chosen technique for focusing attention:

Step 1: Taking Control

We tend to be overly reliant upon parents, teachers, bosses, counselors, therapists, coaches and others when trying to manage or improve our own lives. We often place too much stock in what these people can do for us, and too little stock in what we can do for ourselves. In this exercise you are your own ideally qualified coach. After all, you know yourself better than anyone else does. Simply set the intention to develop your chosen technique with power and authority.

Step 2: Brainstorming

Reread the description of your chosen technique several times. Each time you do this, consider activities that might help you develop it. *Is there an assignment or challenge that you might give yourself? Are there common opportunities in your everyday life to work on it? Can you think of adventurous experiences that might force your growth in this area? Are there particular relationships in which you might work to develop it? Are there resources available to help you with your chosen technique?* Take your personal interests, hobbies and responsibilities into account. List every activity that comes to mind. Weak ideas will give rise to strong ones. Come up with at least ten possible exercises or activities. Remember, coaching is a serious job—even when you are coaching yourself.

STEP 3: DEVELOPING YOUR TECHNIQUE

Circle the activities or exercises that interest you the most or that seem best suited to support your growth. Prioritize them. Activity #1 is the activity that seems the most interesting or powerful. Create an official "Technique Development" page (see Figure 3) on which you list your chosen technique and activities. Copy the description of the technique onto this page for quick reference. As new activities come to mind add them to your list. Consider keeping a simple note of things that you learn or notice each day during this process.

STEP 4: EXERCISE

Each morning *take no more than five minutes* to read through your "Technique Development" page and think about what activity or exercise you will assign yourself today. Also, think back over the previous day. *What strides or progress did you make? What challenges did you run into? How might you have enjoyed the process more? What will you do differently today?* This is the "active reflection" process that was explored in Exercise 2a. It is an extremely powerful technique for personal development. If you seriously apply yourself to five minutes of active reflection each morning, you should experience greater self-awareness and an increased focus of attention within seven days. You may then decide to keep working at it, choose a new technique to develop, or move on to Chapter 4.

TECHNIQUE DEVELOPMENT
My Chosen Technique for Focusing Attention:
"Questioning"

The average four year old asks more than 400 questions a day. In the process the child's intellect, lucidity, and focus develop at a remarkable pace. By asking thoughtful questions, we temporarily stop projecting our own thoughts and ideas all over the place and allow ourselves to gaze directly into the vast unknown. Spending more time with questions and less time with answers, we manage to increase our lucidity while flexing our focus at the same time.

Possible Activities

ACTIVITY #1: Come up with an interesting "question of the day" each morning and survey people about it during the day. *(What's the most important thing that most people never learn? Who's the most influential person in your life and what made him or her #1? What does the word "spiritual" mean to you? What one change would make the world a better place? And so on.)*

ACTIVITY #2: Try to learn something new about someone by asking a thoughtful question.

ACTIVITY #3: When people ask me for advice about something, ask them about their own thoughts first before telling them mine.

ACTIVITY #4: Keep a scrap of paper with me all day and whenever I think of an interesting question, write it down.

ACTIVITY #5: Ask other people what they think are the most important questions in life.

ACTIVITY #6: Come up with some interesting questions about things that I think I know all the answers to.

ACTIVITY #7:

ACTIVITY #8:

ACTIVITY #9:

ACTIVITY #10:

Daily Notes or Interesting Discoveries

DAY 1: I find it hard being quiet and patient when other people stumble around trying to explain their thoughts.

DAY 2: Even boring people can be interesting if you ask them the right questions.

DAY 3: Asking other people for their thoughts or opinions on things seems to help build up their confidence.

DAY 4: People seem to be taking me more seriously now that I am taking them more seriously.

DAY 5:

DAY 6:

DAY 7:

FIGURE 3.

Example of Creating "Technique Development" Pages for Focusing Attention

Essential Questions

Take a few moments to ponder the following questions. Allow yourself to come up with at least three answers to each question as a means of self-discovery. Keep a written record of your answers in a log or journal.

- What do all my answers to previous essential questions say about who I am, or where I am in life?

- From this point forward, what self do I most wish to create?

- What are the most significant actions that I can undertake to create my most desired self and my most desired life?

CHAPTER 4

The Art of Mindfulness

We are what we repeatedly do. Excellence, therefore,
is not an act, but a habit.

—ARISTOTLE, philosopher and teacher (384–322 BCE)

Have you ever had a genuine conviction to change some aspect of your life, yet found it difficult to actually make it happen? Perhaps you recognized that a habit of yours wasn't serving you well. You set out to break it, or replace it with a healthier habit, but your good intentions seemed to lose their vigor as the weeks passed. Maybe a voice inside your head convinced you to start tomorrow, always tomorrow, and the new you remained perpetually one day out of reach.

This phenomenon is not the result of weakness or inability. The mind is like a highly sophisticated computer. It develops programs and routines that automatically carry out your common activities, thoughts and behaviors. These programs run subconsciously, without your awareness. They often continue to operate long after their usefulness has passed, and come to inhibit new aspirations that arise as you mature.

By developing a discipline of *mindfulness*, you learn to take charge of the subconscious programming that guides your everyday behavior. You learn to write and rewrite your own mental programs, aligning them to support your latest goals, intentions, ambitions and pursuits.

For one interested in developing this art, three topics are of value:

1. **The Nature of Mind**—Understanding how the mind's machinery operates.

2. **Mental Programming**—Recognizing how patterned behaviors are formed.

3. **Developing Mindfulness**—Learning to align subconscious programs with conscious intentions.

The Nature of Mind

Your mind is a primary resource used in shaping your life. It guides your actions, controls your thoughts and beliefs, automates your behaviors, and so on. By acting in these ways, it crafts all aspects of your being—your lifestyle, habits, relationships, opportunities, health—even your physical body. Similarly, it exerts a powerful influence on the world in which you live. To command your life, therefore, you must first command your mind.

Imagine a sculpture that has the ability to sculpt itself. This is, in effect, how the mind works. It has two key parts, *consciousness* and *subconsciousness*. The subconscious region is the *sculpture*. It is passively receptive to whatever knowledge or programming is impressed upon it, much the way clay is receptive to etching or molding. It absorbs and archives everything you know and understand; it houses and operates the mental programs that automate a majority of your daily actions.

The conscious mind, by contrast, is the *sculptor*. It is the part of your mind that pays attention to things, makes discoveries, makes decisions, sets intentions, and identifies itself as "me." Like an artist, it actively molds the substance of your subconscious mind. It is but a small fraction of your overall mind, yet it has the potential to be master and overseer.

In the big picture, consciousness is responsible for bringing about dynamic changes in your being. Subconsciousness then preserves those changes in a static continuity. This dual nature is the key to your mind's ever-adapting, constantly evolving power. When you learn to make use of it, life itself becomes an art form.

Consider the case of Marla, an average child. In her earliest years, the artist of Marla's conscious mind does not yet have much substance to work with, as little knowledge or programming have accumulated in her subconscious mind. She therefore spends much of her time simply gathering information through her senses and downloading each little nugget of knowledge and experience directly into her subconsciousness.

Marla is not yet able to reason or logically distinguish between good and bad, useful and harmful, fact and fiction. She is, however, able to develop basic *associations* with the nuggets of knowledge that she gathers. For example, she may positively associate "kisses" with a warm feeling of affection and negatively associate "soapy water" with the discomfort of stinging eyes. She learns to respond to things accordingly, based on the feelings or consequences that she associates with them. In this manner, she develops patterned behaviors which serve as a form of mental programming.

Marla's associations are highly subjective, influenced by her unique experiences and perceptions. While her older brother learned to perceive "dogs" as fluffy and loving, she associates them with biting and growling. She behaves in an erratic and frightened manner toward every dog that she comes into contact with, putting even Creampuff, the family's playful puppy, on edge. This behavior creates a self-fulfilling prophecy about the untrustworthy nature of "dogs," shaping her life accordingly.

Each nugget of knowledge and each association that Marla accumulates—subjective though it may be—is automatically downloaded into the receptive form of her subconscious mind as a simple "truth." These truths quickly build up, forming a kind of mental blueprint that defines her sense of reality. It profoundly influences her perceptions of everything—of life, people, relationships, and so on. Therein, it shapes the way she interacts with everything.

By the age of eight Marla's subconscious blueprint describes her personal reality in great detail. She is not a math person. She is a princess, at least when daddy is around. Technology is complicated; classical piano is easy. Marriage lasts until grownups get into big arguments. Touching oneself between the legs is bad, especially in the bath tub. Boys are athletic, and many of them are more intelligent than girls can ever be. Girls are sweet, except when they are alone together. And so on. These are the laws that govern Marla's universe. Many of them will serve as guiding truths to carry her through life, for better or worse, until her dying day.

By this magical age of eight, however, Marla's mind has developed a new capacity: *critical thinking*. This allows her to filter truths before they are downloaded into her subconscious mind. It can also rewrite truths that have already been downloaded. It can make rational choices, develop morals and values, and even consciously create mental programs that support Marla's dreams and ambitions.

During the course of each new day, fresh nuggets of knowledge and information are stored in a kind of short-term memory bank where they can be analyzed, sorted, and then *selectively* downloaded. Through thought and conversation, Marla sifts through the accumulating information, analyzes it, discards useless bits, and synthesizes relevant bits into greater understandings. She now has much more conscious control over what *is* and what *is not* downloaded to her subconscious form.

Upon going to sleep, a day's collection of information is further processed in her dreams. More bits of information are downloaded while others are discarded. By morning, Marla's short term memory is free and ready to accumulate fresh information. A bad night's sleep will compromise this process of course, clouding her new day with tangled fragments of yesterday.

On occasion Marla's "critical thinking" ability may detect a gap or inaccuracy in one of the truths, understandings, or mental programs that she acquired when she was younger. Under such circumstances her critical thinking seeks to correct the inaccuracy or fill in missing pieces. This process can occur consciously, but it most often occurs subconsciously.

For example, though "Santa Claus" was a simple truth when Marla was five years old, automatically downloaded as fact, just a few years later she finds herself questioning Santa's validity. Her critical thinking ability has begun to gather a growing body of evidence that contradicts the factuality of Santa's existence. She now feels compelled from deep inside to actively figure out whether Santa is real or pretend.

In this manner Marla begins to separate the facts that she has accumulated throughout her lifetime into two categories: those that are *real* and those that are *unreal*. She will spend decades reevaluating old truths and reprogramming her mind to serve the more mature self that she wishes to become. In doing this, she will redraft that inner mental blueprint formed during her younger years—the one that describes her own, unique sense of reality.

This is a challenging matter, because over the span of her early life she amassed countless beliefs, associations and programs on a wide range of topics. On the matter of "ice cream" alone, she holds hundreds of associations with joy and delight. Though she may wish to eat less ice cream now that she is health conscious, those hundreds of joyful ice cream associations continue to scoop it into her mouth just the same.

If Marla takes some time to examine her life she will find reflections of her deepest beliefs in everything around her. Her thoughts, actions, reactions, intentions, programs, and emotions have worked together like a top-notch construction team, laboring moment after moment, day after day, to make her inner truth a reality. With little awareness she has used her personal power to manifest every detail of what she believes is possible for herself. Though she may say that this is not the life she has chosen, it is nonetheless a life that she has created.

The beauty of this model is that to change her life, all she has to do is redesign her internal blueprint—her sense of truth about who she is and who she wants to be. The moment she begins the redrafting process her subconscious crew members automatically take up their hammers, saws, chisels, and nails, attending to the reconstruction that she inspires. Using the art of mental programming, she can learn to design and create the self that she most wishes to become.

Mental Programming

A majority of our daily actions are run by automated programs, each of which we have developed over the course of a lifetime. It is a subconscious mental program that puts your clothes on in the morning, guiding your arms, hands, and so on to engage in repetitive actions, thereby freeing your conscious mind to attend to more pressing matters like determining whether *that shirt* matches *those pants.*

Mental programs allow us to respond quickly and effectively to a wide range of circumstances. They make it possible to perform multiple operations simultaneously. They form the groundwork for our specialized skills, both physical and intellectual.

Some of our programming is instinctual, such as the fight/flight response that triggers specific physiological changes when a threat is perceived. Most of our programming, however, is developed through day-to-day living. Chapter 2 on Brilliance examined how we accumulate *emotional charges*, which if triggered, overwhelm our conscious intelligence and force us to *react* with patterned behaviors. These charges are like switches that automatically initiate some of our mental programs. Similarly, *associations* developed throughout our lives guide us to seek out certain situations and avoid certain others—over and over and over again.

As we mature, our programming becomes more sophisticated. We learn to integrate multiple mental programs into complex skills, talents and arts. In driving a car, for example, one must coordinate hundreds of physical and intellectual programs simultaneously in order to arrive at the right destination alive. The conscious mind acts like a conductor, finessing the coordination of these programs to bring about precision results.

Over the years, we accumulate a host of mental programs until much of our daily activity is habituated—automatically run by the subconscious mind. Eventually most of what we do is guided by programs developed long ago. The act of changing or improving aspects of our lives grows increasingly challenging.

Eight basic mental programming techniques allow us to reprogram the subconscious mind, altering habits of yesterday to support the conscious pursuits of today:

[1] DISSOCIATION

By distancing yourself from limiting relationships or from environments filled with reminders of a younger, less mature self, you create opportunities to wipe the slate clean and begin anew. Dissociation is the act of removing yourself from conditions that trigger attitudes or behaviors you no longer wish to embody. Change the world in which you dwell and you change yourself as well.

[2] SATURATION

Like a potato in a pot of soup, you absorb the ingredients by which you are surrounded. The friends and mentors that you hang out with, the activities you engage in, the subjects you study, and the media that you expose yourself to, all fill your head with raw material for subconscious programming. Saturate yourself with people, information, and experiences rich in the qualities that you desire. Choose reading materials, books on tape, and movies that elevate you to the self you wish to become. Corresponding mental programs form all by themselves.

[3] AFFIRMATION

As the hours of each day pass, you absorb information through your senses, accumulate it in short term memory, and then process and download it during sleep. The closer to bedtime the exposure, the more pure and direct the download is. The last fifteen minutes before sleep each night, once the lights are out, think or talk about positive intentions, visions, and statements describing the *you* that you wish to become. Think of them in the present tense, as if they are already true. Old beliefs can be quickly reprogrammed in this manner. Spend the days that follow acting as if your intentions have come true. Think and behave the way that *new you* would think and behave. The dawn of a new reality soon emerges.

[4] REFLECTION

Information accumulated in short term memory need not wait for sleep to be downloaded. By pondering ideas, writing, journaling, or conversing with others to sift through the lessons of a day, information is actively downloaded into the subconscious mind. Spend time thinking and talking about the things you wish to understand as well as reflecting on your progress in developing skills and talents. By thinking about what you do, you craft and fine tune the programs that run your life.

[5] REPETITION

You can manually program your mind to master various functions by simply repeating thoughts, behaviors, or actions. Practice is the key to precision programming. The more often you do or think something, the more it becomes a part of your being, for better or worse. Spend less time engaging in the activities of a self you no longer wish to be, and more time doing the things that bring out the new, desired you. By doing it repeatedly, you eventually become it.

[6] POSITIVITY

It is easy to think or say things in terms of negative statements such as, "I just can't get out of this rut; my life is going nowhere." The way we speak and think directly affects the way we program ourselves. Stop yourself when you recognize a negative statement and phrase it instead in a positive light. "It's time for a fresh start, time to make something happen. Life is wide open before me."

[7] IMAGINATION

By reaching beyond the known truths of your everyday world, you plant seeds in the mind for possible futures. Whether guided by your worst fears or your highest hopes, that which you imagine takes root in the subconscious mind. Dreaming and talking about it, or artistically expressing it, you water and nourish it. Next thing you know, the dream has begun to take shape in your real, everyday life. Chapter 8 explores *imagination* in greater detail.

[8] HYPNOSIS

There are circumstances under which one's conscious self-control can be shut down, reducing even an adult's mind to the level of a toddler's. Known as *hypnosis*, this state is brought on by an overload of information. Many of us spend much of our time in a semi-hypnotic state, overwhelmed by stress, anxiety and other phenomena. All it takes is a little additional sensory input—the mesmerizing effects of television or peer pressure—and whammo, we're hypnotized. *Information is suddenly downloaded to the subconscious mind directly, without filtering, analysis or reason. We become highly susceptible to the suggestions of other people, media, and so on.* Used intentionally, hypnotherapy or self-hypnosis are powerful methods for reprogramming the mind. Used unintentionally, hypnosis opens the mind to all sorts of unauthorized programming.

Consider the case of Ben, an ordinary urban fifteen-year-old. It is Monday morning, 6:30 a.m. Ben's alarm clock sounds, waking him for school, though the mental processing of a night's sleep is not yet complete. Head filled with dream fragments and grogginess, Ben shuffles to the kitchen for breakfast in a semi-hypnotic state, highly suggestible. He flips through the pages of *Tough-Guy Magazine*. Aggressive advertisements and images are directly imprinted into his subconscious mind as simple truths about masculinity.

After a shower he finds himself a bit more conscious and heads off to school. As always, first period Algebra overwhelms him with a bit too much information a bit too early in the day. Over the last few months, Ben has developed a simple subconscious association of "drowsiness" with the class and automatically enters a mild state of hypnosis the moment his rear end hits the seat.

Today Mr. Hanson demonstrates the quadratic equation. Ben stares blankly at the board. Hypnotized, his critical thinking ability has shut down, and thus he has no analytic mind available for Mr. Hanson's rather articulate description. Instead, Ben thinks to himself, "I don't get this." He repeats the statement over and over again in his mind, imprinting it directly into his subconsciousness as a fact, without any reasoning in the matter. This fact will hold true for the rest of his life.

At lunch time Ben hangs out under the bleachers with a group of buddies. One of them—the leader of the group—lights a cigarette and begins to smoke. He lets it hang there between his lips, trying to look cool. He shoves another cigarette into the corner of Ben's mouth, sparks a lighter and says, "Inhale." The combination of this shockingly forward action, the sudden glow of the flame there before Ben's eyes, and the immediate anxiety rising inside, catapult Ben into a state of hypnosis once again. "Inhale," his buddy repeats. The suggestion is received directly by Ben's subconsciousness and causes him to inhale.

Within twenty minutes Ben finds himself in the vice principal's office, driven into hypnosis yet again by an overload of thoughts, feelings, and a bunch of authoritative words coming at him like, "idiotic," "disrespectful," and "suspended." These words are directly imprinted in his mind, descriptors of himself that he had no opportunity to filter or modify. Tears emerge in the backs of his eyes as he steps out of the vice principal's office—an attempt by his intelligence to release the overload of distress and anxiety that has by now escalated to a climax.

He suppresses these tears and walks home to the apartment feeling lost and defeated. In an attempt to "get it out of his system" he plugs in his favorite video game, *Killshot*. He plays it for two hours in a deep state of hypnosis, prowling the streets of a festering downtown cityscape as he shoots bad guys, good guys, and any guys he can find. It seems to take his mind off the day until mom gets home.

After a hostile lecture similar to the one that took place in the vice principal's office, Ben is informed that he will not be allowed to experience the two hours of nightly television and commercial programming that are his usual respite before bed, nor will he be allowed to listen to the dark and degrading music that has helped to lock him in a general state of loathing.

At the end of his day, Ben lies in bed brooding about all the things that seem to be going wrong in his life. As he crosses into sleep his mind begins processing the day's accumulated information through dreams. The thoughts that Ben had about all the things going wrong in his life are among the most powerful and influential programming cues of his entire day, since they have spent the least amount of time stored in his short term memory. These thoughts will have a tremendous impact on his subconscious programming during tonight's sleep. They will ensure that his life continues to go "wrong."

We are, in good part, that which we are exposed to. The ability to shield ourselves from messages and forces that surround us—ones that might otherwise contribute to our mental programming—is essential to commanding our own lives.

If Ben had some understanding of the processes by which he is programmed, how might he have altered some of his daily actions or choices? How might he have defended himself against the various forms of unauthorized programming that occurred throughout his day? What self might Ben have consciously set out to create given the authority and programming skills to do so?

Developing Mindfulness

One of the most extraordinary aspects of the mind is its ability to subconsciously run itself with little to no conscious input whatsoever. You can allow childhood, random daily experiences, other people, media, and advertising to write your programs for you, and then simply ease back for the rest of your life and let these programs run the show. This is, in fact, how many of us unwittingly live our lives. We think that because our eyes are open and our limbs are moving that we are in conscious control.

In the end, this passive life will lack the power and meaningfulness of an existence more intentionally lived, yet it is bound to be an interesting voyage—heavily subject to the ebb and flow of external tides.

More extraordinary still is the mind's ability to consciously program itself, adapting its mental software to promote the fresh and vital aspirations of an ever-evolving you. Mindfulness is the art of actively sculpting your own mind as a means of sculpting your life. Using the natural mechanisms of mental programming hardwired within, you unleash an extraordinary power that is available for the business of ongoing personal development.

The following story of Mara, age twenty-five, serves as an example of how one can snap out of the bad dream that fills her days and awaken that vital, self-creative artist within.

November 4, 2008. The United States of America elects its first African-American President, Barack Obama. Mara sits before the television weeping as Obama gives his acceptance speech, her beliefs of a lifetime suddenly upended. The world she thought she lived in is no more. Over and over, the words of a childhood teacher echo in her mind, words that Mara had never taken seriously until now.

"You have a powerful mind, my dear," Ms. Richardson had said. "Please put it to use. You could be president some day. You could change the world for us all."

The next morning, Mara wakes up to a warm, yellow sunlight beaming through the tattered curtains at her bedroom window. She gets up, rips the curtains away from the curtain rod, and gazes up past the brick building across the way to glimpse a small sliver of blue sky. "That's all the sky I need," she says, and claps her hands together confidently. "Let's get moving, baby."

Before she knows where the time has gone, she finds herself waving goodbye to her ten year-old daughter Sierra, having walked her to school. She takes a moment to glance about the yard at all the children heading off to class and thinks to herself, *I wish I could go back to school.* The memory of a library field trip long-ago comes to mind. She recalls the warmth with which the librarians had treated her.

Mara feels strangely moved by this memory. Despite the many things she ought to be doing during her day off from work, she decides to take a bus to the local public library. She ponders Ms. Richardson's words of encouragement and sets out to find a book on the topic of *the mind.* Several self-help books seem to leap off the shelves into her arms.

The librarian soon issues her a library card and, in hearing about Mara's daughter, recommends some encouraging and inspirational books for Sierra as well.

Not two steps out of the library, Mara finds herself engrossed in one of the children's books. She sits down on the staircase to give it her full attention. Chapters sweep by as a little girl deep inside her finds encouragement that has been long overdue. There on the staircase a sense of hope and inspiration saturates Mara's attention.

By mid afternoon, hungry and thirsty, Mara turns the last page to finish the first book she's read in a decade. She places it in her bag with the others, pulls out a peanut butter sandwich with berry preserves and then heads back to Sierra's school.

They meet up outside the front gate and start home together. Along the way, they decide to swing by the local park where they find a large, beautiful limb of eucalyptus that has fallen from a tree.

"It's like a giant slingshot," Mara comments, noting the unusual shape. "It smells so pretty." She is reminded of her brothers and the toys they used to make out of found objects in the woods by their home. "Let's find some nice decorations like this and bring them home. We can clear out our old junk in the den and start something new."

Sierra's face lights up with excitement. She pulls her mother by the hand from one region of the park to another—all the while collecting pine cones, branches and other natural items scattered about on the ground. "I can't wait to put them up," Sierra says.

They carry the various items home, up the stairs and into the hallway only to find their apartment door ajar. They drop everything, rush inside and see that their television is gone. Collapsing in a heap against one another, they lose themselves in a deep cry.

Some time later, when the tears have run their course and Mara has taken to stroking her daughter's hair, she says, "Maybe it wasn't a bad man who took our television. Maybe it was an angel. Imagine that. Lord knows we spent too much time in front of that old thing."

At dinner, Sierra offers a prayer expressing thanks for the removal of the T.V., and the hope that it was given to someone who needed it. After doing the dishes, it's off to the den to find a place for their newfound decorations. They decide to stand the eucalyptus limb up against the wall right where the T.V. used to be.

"Look, Momma!" Sierra hollers, bouncing on her feet with excitement. "It looks like a giant wishbone!"

"Come here, girl," Mara says, fondly opening her arms. "Let's snuggle up and make our wishes."

They sink down in the old, lumpy couch together, all smiles and enthusiasm.

"I wish to be in this year's school play," Sierra announces. "No. *I'm going to be* in this year's school play! No. *I am* in this year's school play!"

"You'll have to get your grades up, baby." Mara removes the barrettes from her daughter's hair and begins to work at the tangles. "And me ..." She thinks about it for a moment. "I'm going to change the world. I am a politician, like Barack Obama."

"How do you become a politician, Momma?" Sierra asks, grimacing against the tug at her tangled hair.

"I start by joining your P.T.S.A. tomorrow morning," Mara declares. "And I go back to school. We're going all the way, girl. All the way."

What Mara doesn't realize is that in the last twelve hours she has already changed the world. Instinctively employing the techniques of mental programming—dissociation, saturation, positivity, repetition, imagination, reflection, and affirmation—all the while avoiding hypnotic forces such as endless hours of evening television, she and Sierra are well on their way to transforming their lives and all that surrounds them.

They fall asleep in each other's arms, minds full of dreams and ambitions. With this, a new mother/daughter ritual is born, that of coming together at the close of each night to share fresh hopes and dreams, and to set their minds on forward motion, rushing up on the heels of the next dawn to come.

Within six months Mara earns her G.E.D. certificate confirming that she has acquired high-school equivalency skills and secures a scholarship to a women's college in a neighboring state. Steadily working the mechanisms of mental programming, mother and daughter break the bonds of apathy and hopelessness that had long been their lot and set out to create powerful lives together.

Mindfulness is the art of empowering your consciousness to rule over the vast expanse of subconsciousness. Through it you train and guide those inner subconscious workers—the programs that carry out your automatic actions—to work according to your conscious master plan. Dismantling the habits that otherwise live your life for you, and eradicating the hopelessness, self-loathing or self-doubt that holds you back, mindfulness drives you out onto open pastures of possibility where you may create the life that you most desire.

By developing the techniques of mental programming, you develop great mental discipline. Gaining control over what your mind is up to at any given moment, refocusing thoughts as they stray into self-limiting, unproductive territories, you awaken the power of consciousness to rule over your life and your perceptions. You redraft the blueprint of your own reality. Meditation can serve as a particularly powerful tool in this process, allowing you to maximize the attention available to your conscious mind.

One of the truly awesome things about mindfulness is that there are no known limits on the extent to which it can be developed. You can have as much of it as you want. In fact, you already do have exactly as much of it as you want. The question is, might it serve you to want more?

Chapter 4 Exercises

Exercise 4a: Increasing Your Awareness

Mindfulness is a state of heightened awareness. It empowers you to recognize what you are mentally up to at any given moment, and then to consciously influence your mind's activities.

To begin this exercise, read through the story on page 72, looking for evidence of the first mental programming technique described on page 68, *Dissociation*. How did Mara and/or Sierra apply it? Repeat this process for each of the other seven programming techniques, using the context of the story to deepen your understanding of each one.

Once complete, reread the story on page 70 and consider some different possibilities for how Ben could have gone through his day, had he been familiar with the eight techniques of mental programming. Rewrite his story in your imagination, or even on paper.

Now take five minutes to reflect on your last 24 hours. *Did you use any of the mental programming techniques? Did you observe anyone else using these techniques? Did you fall prey to any unauthorized programming or hypnotic influences?* Figure 4 displays an example of a chart that you might use to track your various discoveries. In considering these discoveries, ask yourself an important question: *what might I do differently in the next 24 hours?*

By developing an inventory of the mental programming techniques that influence you—both intentionally and unintentionally—you begin to develop greater conscious command over the programs that run your life. Repeat this five-minute reflection process daily for one week, and then proceed to Exercise 4b.

Exercise 4b: Creating Your Own Mental Programs

Note: It is important that you engage in Exercise 4a to prepare you for this exercise.

Choose one of the eight mental programming techniques listed on pages 68-70 that you wish to develop. *What aspects of your daily life will provide you with opportunities for using it? When will you use it? What steps*

Technique	Circumstances	Result
Dissociation (negative example)	Dropping every one of my boyfriends when things start to get deep.	Keeping myself from experiencing real intimacy. Feeling lonely.
Saturation (negative example)	Feeling dragged down by all the gossip and negativity at work.	Coming home exhausted. Ordering in pizza and watching TV until I fall asleep.
Hypnosis (negative example)	Getting bombarded by sales pitches and sneaky tag-team techniques at the car dealership.	Getting home and realizing I bought the wrong car, and paid way too much for it.
Reflection (negative example)	Continually beating myself up, thinking back on things I've done that make me feel like an idiot.	Having a low opinion of myself. Causing other people to have a low opinion of me too.
Dissociation (positive example)	Spending less time with old friends who whine, complain and speak judgmentally of others.	I feel like a weight has been lifted. I didn't realize how draining these relationships have been.
Saturation (positive example)	Carefully choosing movies, TV shows and internet sites that promote qualities I wish to develop in myself; avoiding all others.	Feeling much more upbeat and intentional; have been having very powerful dreams.
Repetition (positive example)	Taking a deep, calming breath before engaging with each new customer; repeating this behavior over and over as a way of treating each customer like my #1.	Within two days this has become habitual. I find I am much more present and considerate of the customers' experiences. They are tipping well!
Positivity and Reflection (positive example)	Thinking back through my day just before sleep, taking time to appreciate the positive moments and subtle gifts that life offered me.	I'm getting much better sleep. I'm waking up more refreshed and invigorated than usual. I'm noticing positive things during the day more regularly now.
Repetition and Affirmation (positive example)	Repeating the following idea many times each day: "I am present in everything I do, and my actions flow from an honest sense of being."	Feeling much more connected to the things I'm doing—even the shopping, cleaning and so on. Find myself surprisingly more productive than before.

FIGURE 4. *Example of a "Mental Programming" Chart*

might you take to keep the technique in your awareness throughout the day? What obstacles may arise? How will you address them?

Once you have listed some answers to these questions, close your eyes. Imagine yourself actually making use of your chosen technique in the next 24 hours. See your actions in your mind's eye as if they are already happening.

The next day, set out to use the technique as much as possible. Take five minutes that night to reflect on how the process went. *Did you use the technique? How did it go? Did you notice any effects in using it?* Take a moment to acknowledge any successes that you had. Now consider whether or not you had any difficulties. Most importantly, *how will you modify your use of this technique in the next 24 hours in order to improve your success in using it?* Repeat this five-minute reflection process each night for one week. You may then consider starting the process all over again with a different technique.

This activity is most powerful when shared with a friend or family member. It's fine if you each choose different techniques. Simply do your daily reflections *together*. This partnership will offer you two sets of experiences to learn from. Your discussion will spark deeper levels of insight.

Part II
Creativity

Human Life is not merely a biological phenomenon, but an artistic phenomenon as well. Through our thoughts, actions, and interactions we make things happen. We use energy to turn ideas, hopes, and dreams into actual realities.

This part examines the nature of human creativity. It presents four arts through which we shape our lives, our relationships, and the world that we share.

Essential Questions

Take a few moments to ponder the following questions. Allow yourself to come up with at least three answers to each question as a means of self-discovery. Keep a written record of your answers in a log or journal.

- What are the biggest lessons that life has taught me?

- What are the most important things that I might hope to say about myself when thinking back over my life at the end of this journey?

- If I could become an expert or authority on any topic or in any pursuit, what would I choose? (List at least three.)

CHAPTER 5

The Art of Cultivation

Ever since I was a child I have had this instinctive urge for expansion
and growth. To me, the function and duty of a quality human
being is the sincere and honest development of one's potential.

—BRUCE LEE, martial arts master and actor (1940–1973)

Growth is an unavoidable part of life. Whether we mean for it to happen or not, our bodies continually nourish and regenerate themselves, our minds continually learn and expand, and our lives continually evolve. We have the power to craft our growth the way a landscaper crafts a majestic garden, or we can leave it to chance, allowing it to unfold wild as the weeds that spread across a vacant lot.

<u>Cultivation is the art of growing things with care and intent, nurturing the very best of what is available within.</u> Anything that grows can be cultivated, including plants, animals, families, relationships, businesses, communities, nations, and even oneself.

Each form of cultivation relies on its own unique set of tools and techniques. In the art of cultivating yourself, the basic tool of the trade can be thought of as a *curriculum.*

Often misunderstood, a "curriculum" is not simply the stuff that is written in a textbook for you to learn about, or a course designed by a teacher. More integral to who you are, curricula exist *inside you. They are like motivating forces deep within that drive you in very specific ways to learn, to grow, to challenge yourself, and to expand your awareness.* Over the course of a lifetime, you work through countless of these inner curricula. They compel you to develop skills and qualities that are appropriate to your age, maturity level, needs, ambitions, and unique aptitudes.

If and when a school curriculum is designed to support the inner curricula that you hold, your learning is optimized because it is *self-motivated*. You tend to naturally seek books, courses, mentors, experiences, and other resources that enhance your inner curricular processes. If you do not hold an inner curriculum in a given subject area, even the finest books and classes will tend to be of less interest or value. Educators must then seek *external ways* to motivate your learning, such as offering grades and rewards, or bargaining with privileges, or getting your parents involved, or instilling fear in you about your potential to succeed sometime in the future.

Take a moment to think back over all your years of schooling. *What were your favorite subjects? What were your dreaded subjects? What were your favorite periods in the school day?* These things were driven by your inner curricula. If recess and lunch made the list, realize that some of your most important internal curricula were best satisfied during these times—your curricula to connect with peers, or to develop physical prowess through sports, or to read your favorite books in a quiet place.

Consider several general categories of curricula that are at play each day inside you:

- **Academic Curricula** Studying or contributing to that great reservoir of human knowledge amassed over the millennia

- **Intellectual Curricula** Developing intelligence, creativity, independent thought, and the ability to process emotion

- **Social Curricula** Connecting with others, developing communication skills, learning to work, play, and interact effectively with others

- **Physical Curricula** Promoting strength, coordination, and health

- **Spiritual Curricula** Exploring existential questions and values and/or developing a relationship with the sacred

- **Holistic Curricula** Developing talents that integrate some or all of the above through various arts, sciences, trades, professions, and so forth

At any given point in your life, you have a multitude of personal "curricula" running inside you that motivate you to master skills, gather information, take on responsibilities, develop relationships, and work through difficult times. They influence your thoughts, actions, and pursuits. You shuffle them around like open books, slowly working each one through from cover to cover. Once completed, you file them away and move onto new ones.

There is an art to managing your curricula in a powerful and intentional manner. By developing mastery over this process, you take charge of cultivating your life. Three topics are of value in supporting this important art:

1. **The Nature of Your Inner Curricula**—Understanding how your personal curricula operate as they influence your growth, and how they sometimes get you into trouble.

2. **Resonant Relationships**—Recognizing how your curricula interact with those of other people, and how this resonance connects you to each other.

3. **How to Cultivate Your Life**—Learning to consciously manage your curricula in a manner that awakens the great potential within you.

The Nature of Your Inner Curricula

We go through many developmental stages over the course of a lifetime. At each point—infancy, adolescence, young adulthood, and so on—there are new things that we must learn and new challenges that we must face. Our minds create curricula that automatically address these matters, thrusting us into situations that force our growth.

Many of our curricula are created and managed subconsciously, below the radar of our awareness. As the possibility for a new kind of growth arises, a specific curriculum is created to address it. Then, each time conditions arise that may support progress in that curriculum, the mind automatically routes attention to it, thereby activating it.

Picture yourself like a cartoon character with a thought-bubble rising above your head. Imagine that inside your thought-bubble is a bar graph of the various curricula running within you at this very moment. Perhaps 55% of your attention is routed toward an academic curriculum on understanding the ideas presented here. Another 20% might flitter about, spinning off on tangential thoughts, connecting these ideas to your actual life curricula.

Some 15% might be directed to a curriculum on managing comfort, hunger, or other physical issues. The remaining 10% may support various other curricula regarding people nearby, pressing issues, or planning curricula for later in the day.

Imagine now that someone nearby trips and falls to the ground, then cries out in pain. Conditions within and around you immediately shift. Your mind automatically routes attention to other curricula, ones that resonate most closely with the new conditions. You may find 90% of your attention suddenly focused on a social curriculum about dealing with others in need.

Through ongoing daily curricula like these, we develop every aspect of ourselves. Our minds often run multiple curricula simultaneously—an activity know as *multitasking*. This allows us to make the most of every situation, advancing the curricula that are best served by the circumstances at hand.

At any given moment we tend to have several curricula actively running within ourselves, regardless of what we are "officially" doing. Our minds manage these curricula by directing varying fractions of our attention to each, cultivating our growth accordingly. The more we understand this process, the better equipped we are to direct our own growth.

The following basic principles govern our everyday curricula:

- At any moment we may carry within us hundreds of curricula—some active, others on hold. Our minds manage these curricula by routing attention to the ones most served by the present conditions. Many of our choices and behaviors are heavily influenced by our inner curricula, sometimes consciously (with awareness) and often subconsciously (without awareness). Curricula drive us from deep inside to address specific issues in our lives, to seek out specific forms of knowledge and information, to develop specific skills, and to put ourselves in specific situations where growthful pressure will be brought to bear upon us—often with some discomfort. This process enables us to continually improve the quality of our lives. The more we understand our curricula, the more effective we are in successfully working them through. Without this understanding, we sometimes work against ourselves.

- We naturally seek the best possible choice in any given situation, reflecting the maturity and resource available to us at the time. It is important to recognize, however, that various intellectual and mental patterns sometimes severely limit the options that we are able to perceive, causing us to identify detrimental actions as our best possible choices. Self-destructive behavior such as suicide is a classic example of this phenomenon at play. Chapters 2 and 4 explored our intellectual and mental patterns in detail, and presented specific tools for improving upon them.

- Our various curricula sometimes conflict with one another and we find ourselves struggling with a choice between them. Eventually the stronger curriculum dominates and a decision is made accordingly. This can get us into a good bit of trouble from time to time as we will soon see. If and when we are unaware of the curricula at play within us, we tend to find ourselves at a loss to explain why we've done what we've done.

- Each of our multitudinous curricula tends to persist until the needs or interests that initiated it have been satisfied. We may attempt to resist one, particularly if it is uncomfortable, yet it stubbornly reemerges again and again. Each time conditions arise that serve its development, it forces itself upon us until the day when we have truly worked it through.

Consider the true story of Carl, age five. It is 8:30 a.m. on his very first day of school. He stands near the doorway of his new kindergarten class watching moms and dads kiss their children goodbye. Some of the parents seem more nervous than the sons and daughters from whom they are separating.

Carl notices a rather meek boy standing alone on the other side of the classroom. He walks hesitantly toward the boy, glancing at the teacher as he approaches.

As Ms. Smith notices Carl and their gazes meet, Carl winds up and slugs the boy. Within minutes, he finds himself in the principal's office.

"I don't know why I did it," Carl cries. "Please don't tell my daddy! Please!"

An hour later, a group of parents find themselves collected in the parking lot. Late for work, they share stories of what they saw, how they saw it, and whether or not the principal's action was sufficient to protect their children from this terrible boy.

"I saw the whole thing," one father says. "He just walked up to that poor kid and slugged him. He had no reason. It was just a random act of violence."

This father has good cause to be upset. Given the "random act of violence" that he believes he witnessed, he now faces a brand new curriculum about entrusting his beloved daughter to First Street Elementary School. This new curriculum is far more important to him than that of impressing his boss by showing up to work on time.

But was Carl's action really a random act of violence? Is he really a terrible boy?

Let's take a closer look at Carl's world, and the curricula that govern it. What the parents, teachers, and students don't know about Carl is that he is the youngest and meekest of three brothers. When he is not serving as a punching bag, he is struggling to protect his belongings, ignore insults, and avoid being blamed for his brothers' mishaps.

Carl's home-life is physically and emotionally unsafe. Today he enters the world of school for the very first time in his life. The number one question on his mind—his number one curriculum of the day is: *Will school be as unsafe as home?* Given the sheer number of people, and the nervousness of parents as they say goodbye to their children, Carl hypothesizes that school is even more dangerous than home.

Anxiety builds inside him as the moments pass, subconsciously pressuring him to do something, perhaps test his hypothesis. Without rhyme or reason, he finds himself slugging another child with the teacher's full attention.

Almost immediately thereafter, the teacher admonishes him for this action. The principal soon repeats the process, and then sends him home. Through it all, Carl thinks to himself, *Maybe hitting isn't allowed at school. Hmmm.*

Without question, his curricular experiment has paid off. He has gathered crucial information about his level of safety at school.

The next day, as Carl steps into the classroom once again, he feels a strange sensation pass through him. His entire body seems to relax.

Confused by the sensation, he stands in the doorway gazing around at the other children.

Billy, the subject of Carl's experiment the day before, notices Carl there in the doorway. Seeing himself in Carl—the boy all alone—he does a surprising thing. He begins to walk hesitantly in Carl's direction. It turns out that Billy's curriculum on effectively connecting with others currently outweighs his curriculum on avoiding physical harm. He finds himself driven to seek out the boy who like himself seems most alone, regardless of the potential threat.

Billy steps up beside Carl and stands there for a moment glancing about. As the boys' gazes meet, he says, "Wanna play cars?"

Each of us has the ability to examine our various actions and behaviors from a non-judgmental point of view, observing the underlying curricula that drive us. By tuning into our curricula and those of others, we begin to recognize the forces at play in our lives, both within and around us.

Resonant Relationships

Every curriculum carries a unique signature, a resonance, the same way that every radio station broadcasts at its own unique frequency. The drive to start a family, for example, or to run a marathon, or to create flower arrangements, or to amass a fortune each has a unique feel, a resonance all its own.

Without necessarily meaning to, we broadcast our curricula all around us and tune into the broadcasts of others. In this way we attract people into our lives whose curricula resonate most closely with our own, or we find ourselves drawn into their lives. Partnering up as either friends or adversaries, or sometimes both, we set out to work through our curricula together.

If you want to know what your major curricula are, take a close look at the people and things around you. You have surrounded yourself with relationships, projects and situations that resonate with your curricula. You have attracted partners, circumstances, and challenges that provide opportunities for growth at this stage in your personal development. As we will see, there is an art to engaging these opportunities in a manner that elevates both you and those around you. Without understanding or developing this art, however, you may find yourself feeling stuck, unsure of how to make the most of the situations you face.

In the case of Carl, our kindergartner struggling with issues of safety, it is interesting that of all the children in his class, he seeks out Billy, the meekest child he can find. This is because Billy's curriculum resonates with his own. The boys are attracted into one another's lives, and quickly form a sometimes-love, sometimes-hate relationship with one another.

Some might consider the friendship between them as a classic example of how opposites attract, in this case "the bully" and "the wimp." But Carl and Billy are not opposites. They resonate with the same curricula, each timid and unsure of his place in the world, unsure of how to get along with others. They are two sides of the same coin.

Whether it is comfortable or not, our most powerful learning and development occurs through interactive growth, partnering up with others to work through our curricula. Common forms of partnership include cooperation, collaboration, competition, and conflict.

Day after day, we find opportunities to become more conscious of our curricula, to work through them, and to move onto new ones. For example, we may use oppressive or challenging circumstances to inspire a period of skills and attitude development. If we do this, we can empower ourselves to rise above our oppression and challenges. We can elevate ourselves. Our resonance tends to gradually shift in the process, matching our ever-evolving maturity, interests and empowerment. By working through our curricula and moving onto new ones, we find ourselves attracting people, circumstances, and situations of increasing sophistication into our lives.

When a person's curriculum in victimhood has been overcome, he stops getting beat up. He no longer resonates with the flip side of his coin, the victor. They no longer attract one another. In this manner, personal growth dissolves many of our problems by elevating us out of them. We promote ourselves through personal growth and find ourselves presented with new levels of opportunity by employers, mentors, friends, peers, and strangers.

The fastest way to consciously work through a curriculum and promote personal growth is to approach that curriculum from the highest level of maturity available within us. We generally operate at only the midpoint, simply because we have more experience resonating at lower levels of maturity than we do at new, more sophisticated levels. We slide back and forth, rising virtuously and falling immaturely through the slow, enduring process of personal evolution.

By elevating ourselves to the highest level of maturity available within, we can elevate ourselves quickly through a curriculum. This might be brought about by thinking of the most mature people we know or admire, then asking ourselves how they might handle the very situations or curricula that we now face. This process allows us to access wisdom deep within, elevating ourselves to the highest level of sophistication available to us.

In the throes of an argument with her husband, a woman reminds herself of this principle. She tries to imagine how her beloved grandmother would handle the same situation. Quite impulsively, she reaches out and grasps her husband's hand. Hearing her grandmother's voice in her head, she says, "Look at us, honey. We're yelling at each other like the kids do." She smiles. "Let's try something different. Tell me about why you're upset. I'll just listen for a change." In the moments that follow, she comes to realize that he is upset about a bad day at work, not about the meatloaf or the soufflé.

Resisting our curricula or judging them harshly tends to only slow our growth process down. It is best to simply realize that we face the current circumstances for a reason. The key is not to judge a curriculum, not to fight it, but to learn from it.

One does not win a game of chess by simply wanting to win. One wins by analyzing the board and making effective moves. Similarly, we don't fulfill our curricula by wanting them to be over. We fulfill them by taking time to understand them, then taking action to work them through.

Once you have worked a curriculum fully through, it dissolves. For example, once you have mastered the ability to stand up on two legs, you no longer put time, thought or energy into developing this skill. The curriculum is fulfilled.

We are largely unaware of all the curricula we have fulfilled because we don't think about them anymore. We no longer resonate at their frequencies, and thus no longer attract people or situations of similar resonance. We have turned our attention to new curricula, tuned into new channels, and begun to resonate at those frequencies instead.

Try as we might to attract certain people into our lives, if our curricula don't resonate with theirs, these relationships don't tend to take hold. To attract people of higher maturity, we have to elevate ourselves to their resonance. We have to actively take charge of our curricula, intentionally bringing about our desired growth.

How to Cultivate Your Life

The art of personal development is much like the art of farming. It is the cultivation of growth, of being, of life itself. A few basic farming techniques can therefore be quite valuable when setting out in this pursuit.

Effective farmers tend to cultivate their crops in three basic steps:

1. They find or create the conditions under which the desired crops can flourish.

2. They plant the right seeds at the right time.

3. They attend to the ongoing needs of their crops.

If you wish to cultivate something in yourself, or in fellow human beings, these same techniques apply:

1. Create the conditions under which the desired growth can flourish.

2. Provide the right seeds at the right time (i.e., provide experiences and exposure to relevant information when each can be best utilized).

3. Attend to the desired growth by directing attention and resource to it.

If you want to grow a chef, you must first find or create a kitchen, then provide the resources necessary for developing in the culinary arts. You might examine the work of other chefs, ask one to mentor you, experiment with various tools, recipes, techniques, concepts in health and nutrition, and so on. You shine the light of your attention on this exciting curriculum, and the growth of a chef occurs all by itself.

To grow anything in yourself, put yourself in the climate best suited for the desired growth and surround yourself with the proper resources needed.

If you plant yourself in a dysfunctional, codependent relationship, for example, you are likely to grow a dysfunctional, codependent self. If you want to become a mature, well adjusted person, you will need to transplant yourself from this dysfunctional environment into a new environment suited for the self you wish to grow.

When I was a teenager, my drum teacher Pete sat me down and said, "Scott, if you want to be a great drummer, join a band that's out of your league. You'll struggle to keep up for a while, but you'll learn more than I can ever teach you. You'll absorb talent."

Under the right conditions, with the right seeds and a little attention, any form of growth that you desire can flourish.

To effectively cultivate yourself, it helps to recognize the curricula that are currently most active for you. *What do you spend your time thinking and talking about? What kinds of people do you associate with? What situations commonly come up for you? What kinds of struggles do you experience? What books or magazines do you read? What programs do you listen to or watch? What are the lyrical themes in your favorite songs? What are your favorite subjects? What kind or kinds of work do you do? How do you feel about your work? What do you dream about? What are your greatest aspirations?*

All of these things are driven by your underlying curricula. If you write them down on a master list and examine them, you will begin to notice patterns and themes. These are the broad strokes of your current curricula, the center-points of your growth. Keep in mind that they are temporary, that you are always growing, always evolving.

To take conscious command of your own cultivation, take the following steps (Exercises 5a and 5b will guide you through this process):

STEP 1: AWARENESS

List your various current life curricula, including social, emotional, intellectual, work related, spiritual, et cetera, then identify your top three—the most commonly recurring themes. Choose one of these three to work on (see Exercise 5a).

STEP 2: VISION

Think about the growth you desire in your chosen curriculum. Dream big. Consider what *the cultivated you* will look like in this area. Write about it, or create a picture in your mind. Daydream about it. Draw it or create a collage of images about it. Talk to others about it. Revisit your vision over and over again.

STEP 3: NOURISHMENT

Identify the ideal conditions and resources for growing this envisioned, cultivated you. *What services might support your process? Who might want to help you? Who may wish to collaborate with you? Are there specific materials that you need? Information? Other resources? Imagine an ideal school or program specially designed to help someone through your very curriculum. What might that program look like? What resources would they have available for you?* Ask people you trust and admire to help you brainstorm through these questions.

STEP 4: ACTION

Set out to plant yourself in the conditions that you identified and surround yourself with the necessary resources. Whether you see the means for doing so or not, recognize that they are not as far out of reach as they may seem. *There are counterparts to your curricula who want to help you succeed, quite simply because they resonate at a similar frequency and share the same curricula.*

STEP 5: ELEVATION

Elevate yourself to the highest maturity level you have available within yourself. Spend less time with those people who hold you back or bring you down and seek out instead those people who already embody the growth you desire, or are at least closer to it than you are. Expose yourself to books, programs, movies, and other media that are uplifting, and that nourish your growth toward the fulfillment of your curriculum.

Inventor Thomas Edison once said, "If we all did the things we are capable of, we would astound ourselves." By diving headlong into our various curricula, giving them everything we have to give, we reach for that ever-evolving best within ourselves. Regardless of the challenges we face, this personal initiative drives us forever forward.

In the words of poet Robert Frost, "the best way out is always through."

Chapter 5 Exercises

Exercise 5a: Identifying Your Current Life-Curricula

The purpose of this exercise is to help you engage in the science of self. During the first half of the assignment, you will set out to gather a bunch of raw information about the curricula at play within you. The second half of the assignment will help you organize that information in order to gain insights about the personal growth you seek at this stage in your life. It is important not to harshly judge yourself or others in this process, but simply use it as a tool for self-discovery.

Keep in mind that we are physical, intellectual, emotional and social beings all wrapped into one, and that self-discovery opens the door to all these aspects of our humanity simultaneously. It is important to be in a stable and upbeat frame of mind when engaging in this exercise so that you can experience it as a nonjudgmental, uplifting, and inspiring process. If this is a challenging time in your life (emotionally or otherwise), skip the exercise and go on to Chapter 6: Authenticity.

To begin, use a set of index cards or a word processing document to answer the questions in Figure 5 . Read through all the questions; then go through them one at a time in your own order of interest. Use the small boxes at the beginning of each question to number them in pencil in the order that you choose to address them. Jot down all your major answers in words, phrases or sentences that come to mind for each question. The more exhaustive each list, the more powerful the exercise. Work through the various questions over the course of a week or so—on different days at different times. Try to address each one, and feel free to add your own questions. Be honest with yourself. Don't let shame or embarrassment keep you from recognizing an important curriculum that is running inside you. Remember: no one has to see this work but you. *If it feels too intense, seek support or skip the exercises in this chapter.*

Once you have addressed all the questions, go through each list and circle the answers that seem significant to you at this stage in your ongoing development or that identify aspects of your life that you are looking to improve. Ignore the questions at this point. Focus on your answers. Circle the ones that most resonate with you. If the same significant answer comes up in multiple lists, circle it each time you see it.

The Science of Self: Developing a Personal Inventory

Try to provide at least three answers to each of these questions. Use the boxes to note the order in which you choose to answer them.

☐ What do you spend your time thinking and talking about?

☐ What kind of people do you associate with?

☐ Who are your closest family members, friends and colleagues, and how do you spend your time together?

☐ What situations commonly come up for you?

☐ What do you fantasize about?

☐ What kind of struggles or conflicts do you experience (both internal and external)?

☐ What are the top books, magazines or web pages that you enjoy reading; what are the topics?

☐ What programs do you listen to or watch?

☐ What are the themes in your favorite songs and movies?

☐ What are your favorite subjects?

FIGURE 5. *Self-discovery Questions*

☐ What kinds of work, hobbies, arts or projects do you engage in?

☐ What are your top skills and talents?

☐ How do you feel about your work?

☐ What do you dream about?

☐ What are your greatest aspirations?

☐ What holds you back?

☐ What are you most afraid of looking at in yourself?

☐ What gets you really excited, or makes you feel truly alive?

☐ What challenges do you wish to overcome?

☐ What emotions do you most commonly experience?

☐ What are the defining qualities of your spirituality?

☐ What's missing in your life?

☐ Who are your icons or role models and why?

☐ Which movie characters or book characters do you most identify with and why?

Once you have circled your significant answers, copy them onto a new master list. Begin to order them. What categories do they fall into? For example, your categories can be *money, career, challenges, passions, creativity, dreams, ambitions, interests, relationships, communication, sexuality, emotion, health, physical body, balance, spirituality, empowerment, transformation*, and so on. Observe the order in which you chose to answer the questions. This may provide further information about your goals for personal growth.

You may now begin to study these categories—looking for common topics, themes or issues that arise in your inventory of answers. Consider using highlighters or markers to color code the answers that seem closely related to one another. Some answers may fit in multiple categories. Look for two to five major categories/themes that seem to show up again and again.

Finally, create a separate "Curriculum Page" for each major theme that you identify (each color category). See "Step 1" in Figures 6 and 7 for examples. Copy all related answers to their corresponding pages. If an answer applies to several themes, add it to each one. If other thoughts or notes come to mind in the process, add them to the appropriate curriculum pages.

These pages identify some of the major curricula that are currently driving your life. Do not judge them as good or bad. Recognize that they are natural to your stage of development. They exist whether you want them to or not. If you acknowledge them, you then enable yourself to address them and work through them with power. Proceed to Exercise 5b.

Exercise 5b: Taking Action to Cultivate Personal Growth

Using your work from Exercise 5a, pick one curriculum category or theme that you are most interested in working through. It may be something that is holding you back in life, something that really interests you, or something that will improve the quality of your life. Consider starting with a curriculum or area of growth that is not too substantial. This will set you up for success and build your confidence so that you may then tackle a more significant curriculum.

Once you have chosen a curriculum, work on steps 2 through 5 listed on pages 91 and 92. Brainstorm on each one and write out your thoughts or answers. You may simply decide to find a school program to support your chosen curriculum. Then again, you may create a personalized educational program tailored to address your own, specific curriculum. Remember that public libraries offer many free resources. Friends, family members, and mentors can be valuable in helping you think or brainstorm through these steps. Figures 6 and 7 provide sample "Theme" pages.

Once you have worked through all five steps, consider the timeline for your chosen curriculum. *Will this process take a week to complete? Will it take a month? Will it take a year? Will it take a decade?* Don't give yourself more time than you think you need. Don't give yourself too little time either.

Set out to make this curriculum a priority in your life. Challenge yourself. If you truly offer the best of your effort and attention to each of the steps, you might amaze yourself with how quickly your desired growth can be accomplished. Be sure to incorporate the various arts examined in this book when developing your approach.

If you have chosen a major curriculum (one month or longer), write about your process occasionally in a journal or blog, taking notes about your ups and down along the way. Find at least fifteen minutes a week to reflect on your progress. *What might you change about your approach? Which of the arts explored in this book can help you? Are there other materials or resources you need? What might you add to your program?* At this time, give yourself a pep talk. Remind yourself why this curriculum is important to you. Discuss your process with someone who is close to you. In the long run, a few minutes of reflection each week will save you days, weeks, months or years of energy wasted in feeling lost, confused, misdirected or unmotivated. It will drive you through your curriculum to fulfillment.

Curricular Theme: Career Advancement

STEP 1: AWARENESS (answers related to this theme) Hate my job; not enough money to live on; no respect at work; obvious problems in the office that no one is addressing; at the mercy of a disorganized manager; afraid we're going to go bankrupt; coworkers don't take my ideas seriously. Not enough time for the family; no sex in two months; missed Tommy's tenth birthday. Seeing clear opportunities to improve the department; more qualified than my manager; need a raise; good relationship with the owner. Hungry to learn more about management; many ideas on how to set our department straight. Want a better life; want to develop my abilities, but don't have time to go back to school.

STEP 2: VISION I will help to improve my company (or a company more interested in quality and success) by developing my managerial skills, communication skills and leadership ability. I will find a way to share my true gifts in the office, and use them to create opportunities for myself, the company and my coworkers. I will manage my time wisely so that I can spend more of it at home with Cindy and the kids. Family and coworkers will appreciate all that I do for them (for us).

STEP 3: NOURISHMENT Perhaps there is an online management course I can take to give me the skills I need to move ahead. I will continue to develop my relationship with the owner and learn all that I can from him. I'll talk to Dad and learn all I can from his years in management. I'll have a heart-to-heart talk with Cindy and find out how I can better support her at home in these hard times, and how she can support me (on behalf of the whole family).

STEP 4: ACTION I'll make a list of all the things I need to do in the next month to move forward, then work step-by-step to address them and cross them off the list. I'll include important family items on the list. I'll share the process with Cindy so she knows how much our partnership means to me.

STEP 5: ELEVATION I'll make a little booklet with pictures and quotes from Bill Gates, Thomas Edison, Gandhi, Cindy and the kids, and Dad; I'll keep it in my back pocket, and will flip through it many times each day to remind myself of what greatness looks like, and what is most important in life. Maybe I'll even include a picture of myself, with a note of encouragement from deep inside. I'll also include this curricular theme page.

FIGURE 6. *Example of a "Career Advancement" Theme Page*

Curricular Theme: Love and Family

STEP 1: AWARENESS (answers related to this theme)
Keep attracting the same bullying boyfriends—selfish and abusive.

Feel lonelier in love than when I'm alone.

Tired of looking outside myself for love; need to love myself; need to become someone powerful in my own right; need to find a man who loves me in my power and doesn't need me weak so he can feel strong; need to find a man who loves himself enough that I don't have to make up for all he's lacking inside.

Want to be the mom I never had; want my kids to have the dad I never had.

STEP 2: VISION Grandma always said I had the heart of a great one. I'm gonna be that great one wherever I go, even here in this hellhole. Gonna make myself the best me that I could ever know, learning all I can learn, putting everything I can into my health. Gonna rise up out of this poverty with grace and love for those who can't do it for themselves. No more putting people down, especially myself. No more drinking. I'm a great one. I have so much to give, so much love to share.

STEP 3: NOURISHMENT Grandma said I could stay with her for a while. Gonna help her out too. Gonna pay my way. Gonna listen to all the things she keeps telling me I have to do. Gonna trust her. She's the only one who's been there without wanting anything back. Gonna give it back by taking it in. That's all she's ever really wanted. I love you Grandma.

STEP 4: ACTION I will stop dating for a while and start working on myself. I'll drop everyone from my life who takes my love without giving it back. I'll stop trying to get love without giving it back. I'll ask Grandma to help me be more like her.

STEP 5: ELEVATION Gonna be like Grandma. Gonna shine like her. Gonna honor her. Gonna trust her. Gonna learn to trust myself like she does.

FIGURE 7. *Example of a "Love of Family" Theme Page*

Essential Questions

Take a few moments to ponder the following questions. Allow yourself to come up with at least three answers to each question as a means of self-discovery. Keep a written record of your answers in a log or journal.

- How do I view myself, whether positively, negatively or non-judgmentally?

- How am I viewed by others, whether positively, negatively or non-judgmentally? (Ask them.)

- How do I wish to be viewed by myself and others?

CHAPTER 6

The Art of Authenticity

Most of the shadows of this life are caused by standing
in one's own sunshine.

—RALPH WALDO EMERSON, orator, essayist, and poet (1803–1882)

Have you ever secretly felt like an impostor, as if you were playing a role that did not particularly suit you? Have you ever intentionally withheld deep truths about your life, even from close friends or family members? Is there a chameleon inside you that forces you to change your colors from time to time in order to blend in with the people around you? Do you ever compromise important aspects of yourself to maintain the love or respect of others?

Most of us learn early on in life to suppress at least part of the truth about who we are. Wanting to be liked or admired, we create *personas*— social images, or ways of presenting ourselves in order to attract and impress others. We wear these personas like clothes when we are out in the world of people, and learn to leave them on even when we are alone. Over time, we tend to forget about our inner selves there beneath our personas. We grow confused about who we are, or what we really think and feel, or what we most wish to do with our lives.

Authenticity is the art of living your truth without dressing it up or compromising it. By allowing your innermost self to shine through with power and purpose, you reveal your unique vision of what is most important in life. You grasp your deepest gifts and aptitudes, and use them to inspire and enrich the lives of others. Though you do not please everyone, your true self calls to those who admire most the qualities that you honestly stand for. As such, you attract people into your life with whom you naturally and dynamically resonate.

For one who wishes to develop authenticity while nurturing the same in those around him or her, three topics are of value:

1. **The Nature of Reality**—Understanding how you learned to see the world and how your *worldview*—your one-of-a-kind reality—influences the course of your life.

2. **Understanding the Ego**—Recognizing that your sense of identity is much like a suit of clothes and can shroud your innermost expressions of being.

3. **Living in Authenticity**—Learning to shine with power and integrity, attracting people into your life who share the same deep joys, cares, and ambitions.

The Nature of Reality

Imagine waking up abruptly. Imagine finding that you are completely invisible, drifting about in a strange, invisible world.

Helpless and afraid, you cry out.

A mysterious force acts gently upon you. It swaddles you in a soft, invisible material. The softness sets you at ease, drawing attention to the edges of your form. It lulls you to sleep.

Soon you reawaken in the invisible world. You find yourself cradled against a dense warmth, and instinctively suckle at it, drawing nourishment. Meanwhile, strange emanations of light, pressure, and vibration bombard your senses from all around. Overwhelmed, you promptly retreat from consciousness once again.

As the hours unfold, you begin to play peekaboo with the world. You wake up to take nourishment, and to gather little bits of information about the strange things that surround you. You then retreat to a deep, restful sleep. Again and again, you wake, soak things in, then retreat.

Your intelligence begins to piece together the bits of information that you gather. It uses them to create a mental map of the strange world around you. The more information that you gather, the more coherent your map becomes. Much like a puzzle taking form as pieces are added to it, the world grows increasingly recognizable with each new bit of information that is added to your map. Gradually various objects out there become somewhat visible.

The most familiar of these objects is the warm being that nourishes you. She is a large blob that moves about through the world, often carrying you with her. Other blob-like beings interact with you as well. By pointing out important details in the strange world around you, each of these blobs helps you to develop your mental map.

"Nose," says the warm being, drawing your attention to a bulge in her form. As she repeats the behavior over and over again, you learn to recognize this bulge. Similarly, you learn to recognize "eyes" and "ears," then eventually "Mommy" and "Daddy."

At this early stage in your earthly development you are of course unable to read the words on this page. Moreover, you are unable to *see* them. An overwhelming majority of the information that enters your senses is still invisible to you. It has not yet been identified or added to your mental map, so you have no intellectual context through which to recognize it.

Whenever your attention picks up information that you have not yet learned to make sense of, you find yourself temporarily disoriented. It is as if you know that something is out there waiting to be discovered. Family members, friends, and teachers help you to make sense of this new information by describing it to you—pointing it out and explaining it.

"These little black things are words," Mommy says, holding a book in your lap. "I can read them to tell you a story. Listen. I'll point to each one as I read it aloud."

Interactions like these help you to continuously update and detail your map of the world, creating a new context for each new bit of information that you gather. All the while, you learn to align your map with those of the people around you. Identifying various objects and phenomena by name, you agree to map them, thus making them *real*. You also agree to ignore various other phenomena, leaving them off your map, keeping them invisible or *unreal*. In this manner you construct a sense of reality that is closely shared with the people in your life.

As a young child, sensitive and flexible, you sometimes tune into strange phenomena that others do not seem to notice. Because the adults in your life never learned to map this information when they themselves were young, they are unable to perceive it and are therefore unable to help you make sense of it. If you talk to them about it they simply explain that it is not real. In most cases you eventually learn to agree. The information slips away from your awareness, remaining *unreal* to you or, more accurately, *unperceived.*

For example, night after night you may feel vaguely aware of a mysterious phenomenon near your bed, a subtle emanation of energy. It feels strangely relaxing. It reminds you of someone, or something. You tell your parents about it, but they themselves are unable to perceive it, so they cannot help you make sense of it. Daddy just pats you on the head with a smile, then kisses you goodnight. "There's nothing there honey. Go to sleep."

All alone in your curiosity, you may attempt to make sense of this weird phenomenon by routing it through a familiar context, perhaps the idea of a friendly animal. This use of imagination helps you tune into the phenomenon to make some sense of it—though with little clarity. The information is not coming from an animal, yet you perceive it as such.

The next morning at breakfast you share your experience with the family. "I talked to Bobby the unicorn last night," you explain. "He's my new best friend."

Daddy smiles. "You know that Bobby isn't real, right?"

"Whatever," you reply quickly, attempting to keep daddy from changing the subject like he often does. From your point of view, Bobby—or whatever it is that you call Bobby—*is* real. You are not confused about Bobby, but rather about what the word *real* means. After a few trips to the psychiatrist, however, and several months of medication "to help you sleep," you learn to agree that Bobby is not real, nor is that subtle energy emanating near your bed.

The world that you learn to recognize is not the world itself. It is simply your unique description of it. It is but a reflection of your mental map. All the things in your awareness are merely phenomena that you've made sense of in various particular ways, things that you've mapped through life experiences, interactions, and shared beliefs. You therefore hold your own perspective on what is real and true.

Your mental map—your unique sense of reality—is known as a *worldview* or *paradigm.* The more that you learn to adjust it in order to make it correspond with the worldviews of others, the more sensible or clear-headed you are judged to be *by those others.* Of course, worldviews are as varied as religions and political stances. Your degree of "sensibility" is therefore relative to the worldview by which it is being judged.

Imagine now that you are twenty-two years old and rather settled in your worldview. You travel to a faraway country, very different from the one in which you were raised. There you encounter a citizen of that foreign land. You stand before one another gazing out at the same earth, but you see entirely different realities, each the reflection of your own, unique worldview influenced by generations of family lines.

If an appreciation for diversity is woven into your worldview you may form a friendship, using your relationship to learn from this person. If rigid, inflexible beliefs are woven into your view, you may judge this person or attempt to teach him or her to see the world *correctly*, according to the precepts of your personal description of reality. If your view is antagonistic by design, you may escalate into conflict with this person as you attempt to validate the supremacy of your individual worldview.

In the year 2003 the United States of America went to war with Iraq, motivated in part by a clash of worldviews. The U.S. set out to share its view of "democracy" by force, truly believing that democracy is best for all. If the peoples of Iraq use this encounter with the U.S. to form new social agreements, drawing from the worldview of democracy, U.S. efforts will be seen as successful. If the peoples of Iraq ultimately refuse to incorporate this democracy into their worldviews, both Iraqi and U.S. actions will be seen in any one of a number of different ways, each dependent upon the worldview through which they are judged.

No matter how old or wise we get, we only notice a small fraction of what is truly out there, all through the specific context in which we learned to make sense of it. As such, no two people see the world in quite the same way. The greater the difference in life experiences, the more diverse the corresponding worldviews.

The boundaries of human potential are profoundly influenced by our beliefs and understandings about the world—by our underlying views. When we decide that we have learned it all, believing that we see the world for exactly what it is, our maps become rigid and inflexible. We no longer permit them to evolve, thus reducing our potential for personal growth.

By contrast, if we maintain the flexibility of our worldviews, actively advancing them year after year, we continually stretch the bounds of our perceptions. New possibilities regularly emerge for us, keys to unseen potentials locked within ourselves and the world around us. Exercise 6a offers an approach to supporting this flexibility of perspective.

Understanding the Ego

Within moments of birth most human beings instinctively cry out. There from the start our voices are as lively as we are. With age, however, and a rising sense of self-consciousness, we often lose the ability to voice ourselves with passion and expressiveness. Many of us vicariously turn to the great singers of our time, listening in captivation as they hit those impossible notes and belt out the words that *we* mean to say. Echoing our own passions, they remind us of the feelings, hopes and dreams still alive down there, somewhere deep inside.

What would happen if we, like infants, were able to honestly reveal ourselves whether anyone was listening or not? How might our lives be affected if we learned to express ourselves with both the precision and passion of the finest singers? What obstacles might we need to overcome in order to share the deepest truths of our lives with those around us?

Just as each person learns to see the world using a mental map, or "worldview," so we learn to see *ourselves* using a second mental map, the ego. Often misunderstood, the ego is not selfish, arrogant, or opportunistic. It is not something to be avoided or done away with. It is simply a description that you hold of yourself and your identity. It gives you an awareness of your body, helping you to move about through the world without crashing into things. It makes it possible for you to hold an opinion, and to distinguish that opinion from those of others. It brings a continuity to your personality and actions.

The ego is only a map, a flexible description of yourself. It is separate from your actual being, just as a map of the Grand Canyon is separate from the Grand Canyon itself. Under proper conditions it is continually revised and updated, evolving with your growth.

As a young child, your ego may describe *blue* as your favorite color, although the importance of the color blue has little to do with the real you. In actuality each color means different things to you at different times, depending on the unique experience you are having. Sometimes *the blue of the sky* might carry you away. Other times *the green of a forest canopy* might silence you with awe. Maybe *the reds in twilight* take your breath away. Your true relationship with each color is unique to each *real life experience* that you have, defined by how it makes you feel, where it sends your thoughts, or what it moves you to do. *Blue*, as a favorite color, has nothing to do with your true, inner experience of life. It is simply a part of your ego description.

Fine actors learn to put on different identities much the way they put on different clothes. With great mastery they can portray various personas for the entertainment and inspiration of their audiences. All the while, they are able to explore different corners of themselves.

We, too, learn to act early on in life. Hungry for the attention and appreciation of others, we naturally shape our ego identities according to how we are received by our audiences. Many of our likes and dislikes, mannerisms, speech patterns, styles, and various other traits do not arise from an inner sense of being, but rather from the desire to *fit in*. Furthermore, we don't merely *sketch* these traits into our egos. We ink them in. Though these traits only scratch the surface of who we truly are, we soon come to believe that *we are* these traits, that *we are* whatever our egos describe about us. We forget that like actors we can change them the way we change our clothes.

Have you heard the story of Clark Kent, the mild-mannered newspaper reporter who had a big secret? Clark worked very hard to blend in with the people around him in order to lead a normal life. He would not reveal the truth of his extraordinary nature as Superman.

A vast majority of us are living a very similar story. In childhood we created personas much like Clark's to help us fit in with those around us. Unlike Clark, however, most of us eventually forgot about the extraordinary nature of who we were there beneath our personas. We lost sight of many special capacities and talents with which we were born and the predilections that were woven into the very fibers of our being.

Predilections are the drives and preferences of the inner self. They convey a bent toward some individual sense of purpose in life. They are evident in the broad strokes of our interests and tendencies. Emanating from the deepest wells of consciousness they give rise to our special abilities, such as the acuity of certain senses, physical skills, charm or charisma, intuition, genius, or various strengths and aptitudes. If properly nurtured, our deep predilections allow us to access what might be thought of as our own, earthly superpowers.

When caught up in our personas, confusing our ego identities with our actual selves, we have a tendency to stray from our predilections. Like chameleons choosing their colors in order to blend in, we often emphasize a surface appeal over our underlying substance. Sometimes we find ourselves secretly lonely in the social circles that we attract, feeling unable to let our true colors shine through. Suppressing the unique character that we bring to this world and with it, our inherent predilections, we soon lose touch with what it feels like to be *on purpose* in our lives. We forget about our underlying hopes and dreams and lose with them our grandest possibilities.

The art of authenticity provides direct access to that inner being beneath your ego. Through it you learn to reveal yourself with the honesty and enthusiasm of a young child. Soon the gifts and predilections unique to your individual, true nature find the freedom to shine through.

Living in Authenticity

I was once asked to facilitate a weekly gathering of adolescent boys on the topic of "health." In our first several sessions together I tried to establish an atmosphere of honesty and consideration. I hoped to open the floor for deep revelations and shared insights.

At our fourth meeting one of the boys walked in late and seated himself in our circle, apparently out of sorts. Pablo was the alpha of the group, leader of the pack. The others all gazed curiously at him while eagerly awaiting his typically comical opening remarks. He had an uncanny ability to present the most severe topics with a carefree, humorous tone.

"I think I might be part gay," he said, quite unexpectedly. "I'm wondering if everyone is secretly part gay, but most people are just wimps, too scared to admit it."

The boys stared at him aghast. They seemed to mentally grapple with what he'd said.

"It happened last week," he continued. "My gay moment." He rubbed his forehead dramatically, as if utterly exasperated by the mere thought of it. "Jay and me were at his big sister's swim meet."

Jay was a good friend of Pablo's, perhaps his closest. "I thought you were kidding about that," Jay said.

"There we were," Pablo went on, ignoring him. "All these sexy babes are walking around in their wet little swimsuits. They get up on these diving boards one round after the next, sticking their butts in the air. Man, oh man. In the middle of it all, while I'm working up quite a heat, home-boy here comes back from a trip to the drinking fountain. He's trying to show off to a couple girls, right? He sits on my lap, all buddy-buddy, like he's trying to tease them."

Jay gazed sheepishly around at the others. "It was just a goof," he said. "Pablo picked me up off his lap real fast. He's all, 'get off me you little homo. You're rousing the beast.'"

Some of the boys chuckled awkwardly, glancing around at one another.

"I wasn't kidding about it," Pablo added. "It totally freaked me out."

"Why are you telling us this?" one of the boys said, clearly agitated. "You're a homo?"

"Hold on," Harold said, the largest of the bunch. "Pablo's whole story is about being surrounded by hot girls. I bet right then a leaf could have landed on his lap and the same thing would have happened." He scratched his chin pensively. "I mean, I was riding with my brothers to church once in Jose's old convertible. We're cruising up the dirt road to the parking lot, and *surprise*. The creature starts to stir. I'm trying to cool myself off before anyone notices, but the harder I try, the worse it gets. I'm like, *why is this happening now?* I'm freaking out about it like Pablo. But Jose tells me, 'don't stress out little bro. That happens sometimes.'"

One of the other boys, Aaron, was scooting closer and closer to the edge of his seat, as if he was literally on the verge of speaking up about something, pushing himself to the edge of his courage. "You guys ever get curious about how you measure up?" he asked. His question was met with a round of sniggering and laughter, so he continued. "Yeah, but do you ever actually try to sneak a peek at someone without him noticing? And you're like, *wow. Look at that.* But then you feel like a homo?"

"You see, this is exactly my point," Pablo declared. "How many guys have gay little moments like these? But you're supposed to keep them to yourself, right? Instead of 'fessing up about them, you go around calling everyone else a 'homo' just to prove that *you're* not."

This sparked a flurry of argument and conversation. The topic soon morphed away from sexuality, onto an exploration of deep-seated fears, insecurities and shame. Each story that was told had an increasing vulnerability to it, as did the responses. Piece by piece, the boys helped one another to reexamine various disparaging things that they had come to believe about themselves. In doing this, they spontaneously erased old, outdated bits of identity held in their egos, and replaced them with new sketches of the more mature selves that they were rapidly creating.

Pablo's frankness had opened a door. In the spirit of authenticity the boys shifted into a deeper level of honesty and intimacy with one another. As for those few who chose not to join in, it should not be surprising that they seemed the most uneasy and deeply tense of the bunch, brooding beneath their cloaks of invisibility.

Authenticity is the art of truly revealing yourself regardless of how you will be judged by fellow human beings. Overcoming the urge to compromise yourself in order to be liked, you take a stand for the inner ideals and ambitions that you most wish to cultivate. People of like kind are attracted into your life accordingly, drawn by the spirit that they see thriving in you.

As a fringe benefit, authenticity tends to be highly contagious. When you honestly reveal yourself to those in your midst you often encourage or inspire them to do the same. Together you soon establish an atmosphere of intimacy, inviting each other's true colors to shine through.

The key to developing authenticity comes in recognizing that you have independent operating systems that run inside you. Your *ego* runs an operating system known as *judgment*; it approaches life through the lens of good and bad, right and wrong, me and not-me. By contrast, your inner self runs the operating system of *authenticity*; it approaches life through the lens of honesty and directness.

When we are born we naturally operate through authenticity. We immediately reveal our thoughts and feelings about each new experience as it unfolds. With the development of our egos, however, we become *self-conscious*. Influenced by the reactions and judgments of others, we learn to withhold our naked expressions of self. We gather comprehensive notes about the attributes and behaviors that are either pleasing or displeasing to others. These notes form the groundwork for our second operating system, *judgment*, which enables us to engage with those around us in a likable or unlikable way, and to get what we want or need from them.

Judgment operates by distinguishing things as positive or negative, strong or weak, true or false, correct or incorrect, healthy or sickly. It sketches these distinctions into our mental maps and then motivates us to act accordingly. Unfortunately, many of us get overly caught up with right and wrong, or "perfection," and soon become crippled by the fear of making "mistakes." We spend increasing amounts of time and energy avoiding mistakes, or hiding them, or blaming others for them, or rigidly defending them. Yet mistakes—and our honest self-reflections on them—are essential to learning, to growth, and to updating our sense of right and wrong.

Authenticity, our underlying operating system, is concerned with honesty and evolution. It seeks to recognize people for who they really are, acknowledging their likenesses and differences. It drives us to reveal ourselves with power and integrity, promoting the truths, dreams and ambitions that we are most called to realize. It navigates the waters of success and failure alike with its sights set on learning, growth and expansion.

Each of these these operating systems is of great value, but a balance must be maintained. If we overemphasize authenticity our social structures tend to weaken or destabilize. If we overemphasize judgment we become egocentric—selfish in our actions and rigid in our thinking. 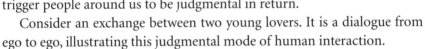 Most of us are prone to this second form of imbalance. We run a continual stream of nit-picky judgments in our heads about ourselves and others, often rather mindlessly. They slip out through our words and actions and trigger people around us to be judgmental in return.

Consider an exchange between two young lovers. It is a dialogue from ego to ego, illustrating this judgmental mode of human interaction.

Wally arrives forty-five minutes late to pick up his fiancée for a movie. As she opens the door, he says, "geeze, the freeway was a mess. Come on. If we hurry, we'll only miss the first few minutes."

Claire grabs her coat, but hesitates. "I should have expected this," she says. "The movie started two minutes ago."

"Don't stress out, babe," Wally says. "You get so uptight." He smiles at her. "The great thing about movies is that they play them over and over again. We can still catch the next show."

"I have to *work* for a living." Claire steps outside and closes the door, then reaches into her purse for the keys. "That means being responsible. Getting a good night sleep. Waking up early enough to have a healthy breakfast. Showing up at the office on time." She sighs and says, "If only I had the luxury of living *the artist's life*. Then I'd say, 'heck, let's drive to Vegas.'"

"Don't go acting like that, like I'm just a flake," Wally replies. "My paintings give people a little meaning in this rat-race of a life. Besides, I make more money as an artist than you do filing papers and answering phones.

I'll have us in a home of our own within a year. Then you can have that baby you're always talking about. You'll never have to work another—"

"Enough," Claire interrupts. "Are we gonna see the movie, or what?"

Throughout this exchange, both Wally and Claire skate around the surface of a much deeper issue. Neither is willing to look at the subject directly, nor are they willing to consider the validity of one another's perspectives. Instead, they make flippant judgments and assumptions. Bound together by great sex, an engagement ring, and the hope of a better life sometime in the future, they nonetheless manage to deprive themselves of experiencing true intimacy together.

A life lived predominantly according to our judgments about ourselves and others tends to be quite complicated, as there is a persona to defend, lies to maintain, truths to deny, and a general sense of confusion as to what is best. By contrast, an authentic life tends to be quite a bit simpler. You reveal yourself through choices and behaviors that are honest and true, and trust that the consequences will lead to progress.

Consider an exchange between the same young lovers in the exact same situation as the preceding story. This exchange, however, illustrates the authentic mode of being.

Wally arrives forty-five minutes late to pick up his fiancée for a movie. As she opens the door, he gazes awkwardly at her. "I'm sorry, babe," he says. "I got caught up painting a sunset. I couldn't put the brush down. I knew I was running late. I just . . ." He thinks about it for a minute. "You mean the world to me. But when I'm painting, I'm in a whole other world."

Tears form in Claire's eyes.

Wally looks away, but soon finds the courage to face her once again. He looks compassionately at her.

She reaches out and takes his hand, then guides him over to a couple of chairs on the porch. "Do you know how much your art means to me?" she asks, wiping her eyes. "It touches regions of my soul that I didn't know existed before I met you. But on nights like tonight, those regions fill up with sadness. I almost wish I never discovered them. Sort of. Not really. I'm just confused right now. We're engaged to be married, but I'm not sure what that means."

Wally stares off at the moonlit landscape. He begins to imagine a charcoal drawing of the scene, but stops himself. "Ever since I proposed to you, a part of me feels like I'm pretending something, like I'm a little kid playing a game." He closes his eyes. "I'm an artist. I follow mysterious rhythms. I'm trying so hard to make them match with yours, but when the brush starts flowing I feel the truth of my life pouring through me in a language all its own. I see you loving my art, admiring me for it. I see you hurting, too."

"Yeah." Claire smiles, wiping more tears from her eyes. "It's funny. You're actually an inspiration to me in that. My work is just a job, something I do to make money. The work that really calls to me is the work of being a mommy. Sometimes I wonder if I'm with you because I know that you can give me that. You've got great genes, and you're gonna make a fortune with your talent. Deep down, I love you so much, but on nights like tonight I feel unimportant. Am I supposed to rely on you to help me feel important? Am I gonna need the same from my kids? Is that how it's supposed to work?"

"I don't know," Wally says. He takes a deep breath, and finds himself intoxicated by the sweet smell of herbal shampoo in her hair. "We've got eleven months until the big date. Let's take some time to really think this through. Maybe we can find that balance."

"We have to figure out what the deal-breakers are," Claire says. "Where can we honestly compromise? Where can't we? Where does that leave us?"

Without judging or assuming anything of each other, Claire and Wally face the truth of their predicament together in partnership. Reaching for the heart of the matter, they examine their problems through an intimate revealing of their inner experiences. Their future lives—whether together or apart—will be the better for it, as is the present moment shared.

To be authentic, or to be loved? This is a fundamental human question. By speaking honestly and directly, we risk offending others or turning them away. Yet, what are the costs of living life estranged from one's innermost sense of self? To live authentically, we must be willing to let certain people drift out of our lives, as this is the effect that honesty sometimes has. Given the sheer number of people here on Earth, however, the potential exists for each of us to be authentic and still find ourselves loved for who we truly are.

If and when we are used to maintaining relationships by appeasing others, the prospect of stepping into authenticity can feel much like preparing to jump off a cliff. Yet once we take the step we are often surprised to find that we do not plummet to our social deaths after all. Rather, we deepen our connections by building intimacy, trust, and understanding. We strengthen our relationships by revealing the underlying ties that endure despite our differences. Honoring and embracing ourselves and each other, we awaken a shared sense of freedom and fulfillment.

Often misconstrued, authenticity is not about being an open book, revealing every detail of yourself without rhyme or reason. It is simply the act of openly and courageously seeing what needs to be seen, saying what needs to be said, doing what needs to be done, and becoming that which you are intent on being.

Chapter 6 Exercises

Exercise 6a: The Explorer

Over the millennia human beings have developed many customs for expanding the limits of their worldviews. Sacred rituals, mystic practices, mind-altering ceremonies, and various arts and sciences have allowed us to tap into the vast unknown. Century after century we improve the quality of our lives by unearthing the seemingly limitless possibilities available to us. Technologies arise in this manner, as do artistic, philosophical, and societal advancements.

Begin this exercise by rereading "The Nature of Reality" on page 102, familiarizing yourself with the manner in which your worldview is developed. Take time to consider ways in which you might like to broaden your perspective. *What curiosities do you hold about nature, life, culture, or spirituality? Are there mysterious phenomena that you find intriguing? What things would you choose to study if you had unlimited free time?* List your answers. These interests are your windows into the unknown, places where you are motivated to expand your awareness and understanding.

Choose one interest that most calls out to you from your list. Take ten minutes to do a keyword search about it on the Internet. You may well find loads of interesting and inspiring information to invigorate your quest for knowledge. For these ten minutes allow yourself to be more than just a person sitting at a computer with a vague interest. Imagine yourself as a new world explorer, reaching into the vast unknown through the nebulous substance of cyberspace.

In our earliest days on earth every one of us is a passionate and curious explorer. We search the world for meaning and mystery, uncovering clues, then piecing them together in our minds. Sadly, our inner explorers are sometime defeated by years of schooling, bound to a desk, distracted from following our own interests and setting out on our own intellectual adventures.

Allowing your inner explorer to be reawakened, you may soon find yourself at the start of a quest, suited up with the wide eyes of a two-year-old and the power and faculties of a mature human being. This quest need not take you far from home. Work, recreation and relationships—mundane though they may sometimes seem—can be among the most exciting of frontiers for new explorations. It doesn't matter where your adventures take you, so long as you push yourself to take some *reasonable* risks along the way. Braving mysteries all around as you had done long ago, you reinvigorate your life. You stretch the bounds of your perceptions and possibilities.

Exercise 6b: Nourishing Authenticity

There are three operating states through which we approach our daily lives: *reactivity, judgment,* and *authenticity.* Chapter 2 explored "reactivity," describing it as a state driven by emotional charge and patterned reactions. "Judgment" is a more advanced operating state, driven by the ego. It bases our actions upon dichotomies such as good and bad, right and wrong. "Authenticity" is the most advanced system available to us, driven by our inner sense of being. It transcends ego and emotional charge, and gives rise to our capacity for *brilliance* as described in Chapter 2.

Begin this exercise by rereading the description of "reactivity" on page 32 in order to refresh your understanding of it. Then read through "Living in Authenticity" on page 108. Focus on recognizing the distinction between "judgment" and "authenticity."

Now read one or more of the stories on pages 35, 108, 111 and 112. *When are the characters reactive? When are they judgmental? When are they authentic? How do these different modes of operation affect the various characters and their social dynamics?* This analysis will help you expand your awareness of how these three operating systems influence your life.

Next, choose one of the following authenticity exercises that most resonates with you. Take a week or two to work the technique. By doing this you will internalize it, making it a regular part of you. You may then choose another technique to develop if you'd like. Most of the exercises take about five minutes a day and will strengthen your capacity to live authentically.

[1] CONSIDERATION

While the ego operates through judgment, our inner, authentic selves operate through *consideration*. Rather than distinguishing things as good or bad, right or wrong, we: (a) set out to dispassionately gather information about the issues at hand, (b) take account of multiple perspectives including our own and those of others, and (c) thoughtfully consider the most effective response or action that we might take to address the unique circumstances we face. In this exercise, consider that people always do the very best they can given the maturity and empowerment available to them. For one day, try to halt yourself from judging the behaviors of others. Instead, ask questions that help you better understand the other person's motivations and point of view. Make comments or observations that acknowledge these things. Share a similar experience from your past; reveal your reflections on how it went. Later that night, take five minutes to reflect on how the day went. Consider how you might change your approach tomorrow in order to improve the outcome. See how many consecutive days you can engage in this exercise. A few weeks later, try again. Try to be more effective at it, and maintain it one day longer. *Consideration* is a powerful means of building authenticity.

[2] HONESTY

To be authentic it is essential that we learn to reveal ourselves for who we truly are. Fearing judgment, however, we often inhibit our integrity and true colors from shining through. Begin this exercise by exploring any or all of the stories on pages 16, 35, 108, 111 and 112. Use them to study the common ways that dishonesty and honesty present themselves. Then, each night for a week, take five minutes to think back over your day. *Did you put yourself out there authentically? Did you tell any white lies? Did you withhold information, or sanitize it to please your audience? Did you exaggerate? Did you tell any outright lies? If so, what influenced you to do so?* Do not judge yourself in these reflections. Just work to understand the forces at play inside you. Now, think ahead to the next day. *What do you hope to do differently?* Set an intention to reveal important thoughts, feelings or aspects of yourself with integrity. That night, reflect again. *Were you successful? If not, what held you back? What can you do to overcome these obstacles?* Authenticity requires risk. Reach for it with power.

[3] Recognition

This activity helps you recognize your three modes of operation: "reactivity," "judgment" and "authenticity." Take five minutes a day, preferably in the evening, to think back over your last twenty-four hours. *Do you remember moments when you were driven by "reactivity" or "judgment?" Do you remember moments of "authenticity?" What were the benefits and consequences associated with each? Do your reflections bring up any further judgments or emotions?* Simply take note of your thoughts and feelings. Recognize when and how these three modes of operation play out in your daily life and how they influence your effectiveness in various endeavors and relationships.

[4] Acceptance

The purpose of this exercise is to help you notice and accept the judgments that you hold, then take time to understand how you developed them. Begin by re-reading the brief description of "judgment" on page 110. Then, each evening for a week, take five minutes to think back over your day. *When did you feel judged? When did you judge others? What were these judgments about? Were they related to health, physical appeal, laziness, irresponsibility, selfishness, inadequacy, mediocrity, morality, ability or talent?* Identify the specific forms of judgment that came up for you during the day—whether you were the one being judgmental, or the one feeling judged. Now think back over your past. *When did you learn to develop each form of judgment? Who or what was involved in helping you to develop it? What were the circumstances?* Each day, try to identify a different, major form of judgment that arises for you, and then discover something about its origins. You will begin to notice themes and trends. To truly develop authenticity, you must first acknowledge and accept your judgments.

[5] Ownership

Eleanor Roosevelt once said, "Nobody can make you feel inferior without your consent." Consider the proposition that all judgment is essentially self-judgment. In judging others, *we project our own self-judgments upon them.* In feeling judged by others, *our own self-judgments are ignited.* Free of self-judgments, we naturally address issues from an authentic, non-judgmental point of view; we are similarly unaffected by the judgments of others. Each day for a week or two, try to catch yourself at times when you are judging others. Stop yourself and look inside. *Where do you still hold this judgment about yourself?* You might have to look deep. Similarly, when you feel that someone else is judging you, look inside. *Where and why did you learn to develop this judgment of yourself?* The purpose of this exercise is not to validate or invalidate any judgment. It is to help you recognize that each one presents itself to you because you grapple with it inside yourself. Take five minutes each night to think back over your day. *Were you able to catch yourself and look authentically inside? What did you find?* Set the intention to improve on catching yourself each day, awakening your self-awareness.

[6] NATURALISM

Emotion, affection, and biology are inherent aspects of our humanness. Yet we often teach children to feel awkward and embarrassed about them. Ironically, we then create hang-ups, inhibitions, and perversions that yield the very nonproductive, obsessive, or predatory behaviors that we, with all good intentions, were hoping to prevent. The authentic human being does not feel awkward or ashamed about parts of the body, hygienic processes, sexuality, affections, or emotion. Accepting the full, holistic nature of our humanness without judgment or shame, we find not only that others are less likely to judge us, but that they too wish to overcome shame. In this exercise, begin by recognizing that judgments are often like fairy tales. They are told to us when we are very young, sketched into our egos and worldviews. Make a list of all the natural aspects of yourself that raise judgments for you. Find *appropriate* ways to celebrate and enjoy these aspects of yourself each day. In doing this you will gradually break down the embarrassment that inhibits you from fully owning these natural aspects of yourself.

[7] AWAKENING

By realizing that our ego identities only scratch the surface of who we truly are, we begin to open our minds to that vast, untapped potential within. We invite ourselves to glimpse at qualities and capacities that emanate from our deepest regions of being. We learn to access and employ our inherent aptitudes and predilections. Begin this exercise by creating a list of the greatest interests that you have held throughout your life, starting as far back as you can remember. Create similar lists of jobs, talents, hobbies, dreams, ambitions, and significant relationships held over the course of your life. Examine these lists side by side. You will begin to notice common themes among them that provide a window into your innermost motivations. Revealed there are the broad strokes of your unique path in life. Can you identify one or two central themes? Carve out one hour a day to explore them, to act upon them, and to truly be *on purpose* through them. You may soon reawaken the heart of your innermost self, and with it, the extraordinary life you were meant to lead. If an hour a day seems impossible, realize that this impossibility is based on a story that you tell about your life; its degree of truth is proportional to the degree that you believe it is true. Chapter 8 will take a close look at this matter of scripting your life through the stories that you tell.

Essential Questions

Take a few moments to ponder the following questions. Allow your-self to come up with at least three answers to each question as a means of self-discovery. Keep a written record of your answers in a log or journal.

- What is my grandest vision of what this life could hold for me and those around me?

- What obstacles keep me from fulfilling my vision?

- What might it take to overcome those obstacles?

CHAPTER 7

The Art of Actualization

The road to success is always under construction.

—LILY TOMLIN, actor, comedian, writer, and producer (born 1939)

Have you ever had a great idea, yet felt impotent to actually make something come of it? Do you ever feel inadequate when trying to see your talents or ambitions through to success? Do you ever wonder what it takes to make a dream come true?

Human beings have an extraordinary capacity to imagine possibilities and then turn those possibilities into realities. Evident in the gifts of civilization—*in our arts, languages, sciences, technologies, businesses, governments, and so on*—it is clear that we are a profoundly creative species. Yet many of us only access a smidgen of our creativity.

How might our lives be improved if we were to fully develop our creative capacities? What's the first thing that you would set out to create for yourself, or for others, if you knew you had the power to do so?

Actualization is the art of making things happen. It enables us to see our hopes, dreams and ambitions through to fruition, giving them actual form in our everyday lives.

For one who wishes to develop this art, three topics are of value:

1. **The Nature of Freedom**—Learning how to command your own life and overcome your limits.

2. **Developing Intentions**—Creating your own designs for how the present and future could unfold.

3. **Achieving Actualization**—Willing your intentions into being to creatively make things happen for yourself, your family and your world.

121

The Nature of Freedom

The United States of America is founded on the principle that all human beings have an unalienable right to life, liberty, and the pursuit of happiness. Yet citizens throughout this and other free nations still yearn for liberation in one form or another, struggling with family members, fellow citizens, and life-circumstances in the hapless pursuit of freedom: freedom from debt, from discrimination, from overwork, from pain, from loneliness, from addiction, and so on.

What is freedom? Is it granted to us by our nations and laws? Must we do anything to claim it?

Consider the distressed facial expressions of many hard-working citizens as they ride to work each day in pursuit of the American Dream. Consider the folks who anxiously comb the abundant isles of their neighborhood liquor stores at the end of each long week. Are these people searching in the right places for their freedom? Where is freedom to be found?

Try as we might to claim it in the halls of our capitals, or out on our various battlefields, or at 90 miles per hour on our highways, or in the stuff that we accumulate, or at the bottom of a bottle, freedom exists in one place only: deep down inside ourselves. It is an artistic license that each of us holds over our own growth and well-being. It is expressed in how we choose to use the energies available to us each and every moment, thereby shaping ourselves and our world.

It might be argued that those bound in shackles are without access to freedom. Yet we are all shackled to some extent by the limits and needs of our physical bodies and by our beliefs and life-circumstances. These limits do not stop us from accessing our own bioenergies and therefore do not inhibit our capacity to experience freedom. How we behave in shackles, how we *work* to apply our personal power in the face of limits—this is what determines the true extent of our freedom.

Work is essential to freedom. Many of us mistakenly associate it with jobs, chores, and assignments, but it is far more fundamental to who we are. It is simply *the use of energy for some purpose.* Every single thing that we do, every interaction that we have, and all that we create is an expression of work, great or small. Through it, we share ourselves with the other beings and forces that surround us. Through it, we apply personal power to effect change.

We are all born inherently driven to work, to make excellent use of the energies available to us. In childhood, however, we are bombarded with an endless stream of assignments and activities designed to prepare us for adult life. Many of these tasks hold little relevance to our age-appropriate *work* interests as boys or girls. We yearn to serve as citizens, to assist and thereby connect with others through our work and play, yet we are corralled into isolating academics for thirteen years or more, some of which hold little practical value.

Eventually many of us find ourselves feeling "unmotivated" to do the myriad things asked of us. Parents and teachers struggle to coax and coddle us through this conflict, treating us as if there is something wrong with us, as if we are inherently *irresponsible*. By doing this, well-meaning adults unwittingly snuff many a child's intrinsic drive to work. By the age of ten an alarming number of us come to dislike, resist, or even avoid *work*, which nonetheless remains our most essential expression of being—the means through which we apply personal power to consciously shape our lives.

In taking undue responsibility to motivate us through childhood and adulthood—spoiling our ability to successfully motivate ourselves—our parents, teachers, bosses, and governors tend to inadvertently finesse freedom right out of our clutches. We grow increasingly resentful, blaming them for our own woes until the day when we can rise up and reclaim that which is rightfully ours: *full conscious responsibility over our own lives and circumstances*. Freedom.

We are not pawns at the mercy of destiny. We are more like kings and queens, each rulers over our own becoming. The first step to claiming freedom is to take personal responsibility for what we have made of ourselves and our lives, even under adverse circumstances. If someone else is to blame, someone else is in control. The next step is to take responsibility for all that we *intend* to become. The final step is to effectively *will* our intentions into being—actualizing them. In this way we take charge of our own lives. We claim our freedom.

Developing Intentions

Imagine walking along on a path. Imagine your arms swinging in rhythm with your stride and the feeling of soft earth giving way beneath your every step. Imagine moving at a steady pace, gazing curiously about at things that surround you. Imagine a far-reaching trail stretching back behind you, the trail of your life, a unique succession of steps that have led you through the world to this very moment.

Not far ahead your path drifts off into a mysterious mist. Much like a blank canvass, this mist is the unwritten substance of your life, the part of your path that has yet to be tread.

Where memories are your link to the past, reminders of that trail behind you, *intentions* are your link to the future, projecting into that mist ahead to give it form. Whether you are aware of it or not, all aspects of your life—health, family, friendship, education, work, life-circumstances, and even your surroundings—are influenced by the intentions that you hold. Learning to craft these intentions, you learn to willfully reach into yourself and your world, consciously and creatively acting upon each.

There are six common varieties of intention available to us, five of which are described as follows (the final form, "Storytelling," will be explored in Chapter 8):

[1] MICRO-INTENTIONS

These are the immediate intentions that drive our everyday actions and behaviors, directing our energies toward specific tasks—for example, to stand, to walk, to eat anchovies, to call mom, to write a hit song, and so on. They are often quite spontaneous, yet can bring about significant changes in our lives. Unless we establish routines to secure these changes, however, they tend to be short lived. We soon find ourselves reverting to the condition that existed prior to the fulfillment of this immediate form of intention. *Consider the case of Margo, a woman who decides in midlife to overcome her obesity. She starts by visiting a nutritionist and comes home from her very first session quite inspired. She rampages through her apartment, tossing every fatty, sugary dessert into the trash. Unfortunately, by 9:00 that night she finds herself shamefully pulling away from the drive-thru window of a fast food restaurant with a hot-fudge sundae and French fries.*

[2] STRATEGIC INTENTIONS

Most people are not comfortable or prepared to have major intentions quickly fulfilled. Instead we spread them out in stages over the course of days, weeks, months or years, leaving time to sculpt them, to zero-in and clarify the nature of what it is we seek. This helps us to absorb the overall package-deal tied up with an intention, to truly internalize and integrate it into our lives. A "strategic intention" breaks a major objective down into a series of tasks or micro-intentions that map a course toward the goal. We might begin by setting tasks for things we wish to achieve by the end of the week, at which time a new round of tasks is set. Alternatively, we may strategically map them out over the course of months or even years and then adapt or refine them as necessary along the way. Exercise 7b offers a tutorial on developing strategic intentions. *Determined to lose 50 pounds, Margo joins a weight loss program. She meets with a trainer and other dieters weekly, using a proven strategic plan to methodically accomplish her objective.*

[3] Macro-Intentions

It is possible to fulfill grand intentions quickly and directly without strategizing. One willfully focuses on a general "macro-intention." He or she then allows all the related sub-steps to intuitively unfold accordingly. This form of intention requires tremendous *willpower*, which can be developed through the Art of Empowerment described in Chapter 1. A state of *presence* is also valuable to the fulfillment of macro-intentions, helping one to recognize opportunities that arise as if through luck, coincidence, or synchronicity. The next chapter will explore *presence* in detail. *After months of empowering herself, Margo drops the strategic approach to weight loss and instead sets a macro-intention "to be in excellent health." She focuses unwaveringly on this macro-intention many times each day, and surrounds herself with posters, pictures and quotes that clarify her intention. She even changes her name to Rose, which she associates with blossoming life. She then simply allows healthy actions and choices to naturally follow suit. Conflicting desires frequently arise, such as the urge to grab a handful of chocolates. She does not struggle with them, argue with herself, or count calories. Rather, she willfully refocuses on her macro-intention, then allows the right action to intuitively emerge and guide her behavior. She soon finds herself having strange, chance encounters with people who introduce her to yoga classes, hiking trails, health food stores, and so on. Within a year she not only loses 50 pounds, but constructs an entirely new healthy lifestyle through this singular intention.*

[4] CURRICULAR INTENTIONS

The subconscious mind frequently sets intentions of its own without our conscious awareness in the matter. Working to support our various life-curricula from behind the scenes, our subconsciousness creates "curricular intentions," taking advantage of the conditions at hand by thrusting us into situations that force our growth. In this process it makes use of opportunities in a manner that helps us to develop new understandings, or that fosters whatever it is that we are trying to learn about or work out. Chapter 5 explored the matter of our curricula in detail and presented methods for effectively working through them. *While driving to Thanksgiving dinner Rose finds herself semi-consciously rehearsing for an ongoing argument with her dad. She imagines all the brilliant jousts and retorts that she might offer to the various comments he commonly makes. All the while, her subconscious mind sculpts a curricular intention to have a dramatic showdown with dad. As the evening unfolds, the pressure inside her builds to a crescendo. She pushes him further and further until a breaking point is reached and they finally get to the crux of their long-standing contention. "Why can't you just accept me the way I am?" she pleads. Dad replies, "I'm not the one who doesn't accept you! You're always putting yourself down! Putting the family down! It hurts me so! All I've ever wanted is for you to be happy!" Seeing the honesty in his teary eyes, Rose has a revelation. She realizes that in blaming the family for her problems all these years, she has kept herself powerless to overcome her problems. At long last, she begins to look at herself in earnest.*

[5] EXISTENTIAL INTENTIONS

The preceding chapter examined the *inner self* that exists beneath our thoughts and ego—that realm of consciousness from which our deepest strivings and bents in life emerge. Sometimes referred to as the *conscience, intuition, spirit, soul,* or *higher-self,* this inner layer of our being directs the will without thought or mental interference. It generally does this without our conscious awareness in the matter. Some of our conscious intentions therefore tend to be in direct conflict with these deeper intentions, causing us to trip over ourselves. By learning to notice these subterranean expressions of will—where and how we seem naturally called to apply ourselves—we catch glimpses of our highest wisdom as it emanates from deep within. Recognizing the deeper tendencies embedded in our own personal power, we can work to align our various other intentions accordingly. A sense of purpose and fulfillment soon emerges, pervading our everyday lives. The next chapter will explore this topic in detail. *At the dawn of a second chance in life, fit and healthy, surrounded by new friends and opportunities, and deeply reunited with her family, Rose begins to see in the puzzle pieces of her former life an enduring theme: the drive to unearth that beautiful, powerful self within. Imbued with forty years of first-hand experience in struggling to overcome her limitations, she sets out on a new path—a life mission to help others do the same. She soon finds herself working at a correctional facility for young women, offering the care and wisdom that she has struggled over a lifetime to acquire within herself.*

Intentions are like targets, directing energy toward specific aims. A well-designed intention attracts not only one's own will, but the will and therefore energy of others as well. Strong leaders and successful entrepreneurs are masters of this art, beckoning those around them to focus energy toward clear and unified objectives. The more energy one draws, the more powerfully an intention is fulfilled.

By taking time to recognize, develop, and clarify our intentions, and by identifying the things we wish to be and wish to have, we draw the energies of ourselves and others into specific courses of action and behavior. An *intentional life* is a powerful life. It allows us to *will* possibilities into existence. Exercise 7a offers step-by-step instructions for using all five forms of intention and for integrating them into our lifestyles.

Consider the case of June, sixteen years old. June is one of those young people who has slipped through the cracks of her schooling career without developing interests, passions, or intentions beyond her day-to-day routines. She dabbles into this and that, listens to music, and reads tabloid magazines, but leads a rather humdrum existence.

June's attention, unfocused, is scattered freely about, searching the world for opportunities and connections. One day while listening to a popular song, she notices the intricate way in which a guitar line is intertwined with the vocal melody. Surprised by herself and fascinated by her discovery, she wonders what it would be like to play guitar.

The lens of her attention suddenly narrows its focus, directing her will toward a more specific range of activities. She talks her parents into renting an electric guitar and signing her up for lessons. Within days she writes her first song—the process of which is unlike anything she has ever experienced. It inspires her to set a conscious intention: she will become a songwriter and musician. Yes. That is what she will do.

In the weeks that follow she finds herself having magnetic encounters with other musicians at school, people who have never noticed her before. One day at lunch during a passionate debate about the influence of rock music on society, June and several of her new friends agree to get together and jam after school. Within two days they form a band and set a collective intention to reach out and touch the world with a fresh and vital music.

Her lens narrows once again, intensifying her will as she focuses on a host of related tasks, such as writing songs, practicing scales, studying the masters, and singing her heart out. She and her band-mates soon find themselves rehearsing four days a week. Intent on success, they become more and more strategic in their approach. Within two months they play their first gig—a lunchtime show at school. From the moment that the drums begin to pound and distorted guitars ring out through the central quad, there is magic in the air. Everyone feels it. Students and teachers alike are drawn out of the woodwork, and allow the band to take them on a journey down a mysterious and vibrant path if only for twenty-five minutes between classes.

Encouraged by the enthusiastic reception, June and the boys begin to stretch the limits of their imagination in song-writing. They give one another license to explore ideas that are out of the ordinary and surprise themselves with a new level of sophistication in their writing—leaps that only weeks ago would have seemed inconceivable. They soon elevate themselves out of the *novice* attitude and adopt a more professional air.

Every aspect of June's life begins to shift, taking on passion and serious-ness. English literature class becomes a playground in which June explores creative worlds shaped by artists of the past. She finds herself paying closer attention to goings-on within and around her, drawing connections between seemingly disparate ideas and experiences through her writing. Her own, unique bents in life begin to reveal themselves through inspired lyrics that issue forth from somewhere deep within.

By the time the band performs their second show June has grown famil-iar with a new, more present state of mind. Not only does she play tight as can be with her band-mates, tuning closely into their every nuance, but she collaborates with the audience as well. She finesses the attention of hundreds and draws a mass of will toward a singular intention: to spend time together aligned in creative connection, rising and falling through chord changes and melodies, dancing and cheering, deeply sharing a good time.

June's parents are blown away by the show and feel strangely conflicted about her success. One night over dinner her Dad comments, "I don't want to burst your bubble, honey, but do you know what percentage of kids ever make it big in rock'n'roll?"

"No Dad," June replies. "What percentage?"

"Well…" He swallows awkwardly. "I don't know the exact statistics, but the outlook isn't good."

"You don't even know what I'm reaching for," June says. "How could you possibly have statistics for something when you don't even know what it is?"

June's story is not unique. We are all musicians of a sort, each playing the instruments of our intentions. Like members of an orchestra covering the globe, we offer daily expressions of personal power through our work, contributing to the great symphony that we call *society*. Through successes and failures and cheers and cries and everyday goings-on, our music radiates from this little corner of the cosmos telling the story of who we are, how we relate, and what we intend for ourselves individually, as families, nations, and one shared world.

Sometimes we find our intentions in exquisite harmony with one another's. Other times we find our intentions in shrill dissonance. By learning to listen with trained ears to those around us we make an art of building harmony, of weaving our rhythms and melodies within that greater orchestra of which we are but one small part. In this manner we learn to tap the abundance of resources and energies all around us. Therein, we find the power to actualize our great aspirations.

Achieving Actualization

Each moment of our lives is spent at sail on an ocean of possibilities. Our hopes, dreams, and ambitions are all out there awaiting our pursuit, as are countless other prospects that we have yet to imagine. *Actualization* is the art of catching the wind, of seeing our possibilities through to fruition. By developing clear and focused intentions, then willing those intentions into being, we turn possibilities into realities. We create the actual lives that we most wish to lead.

There are three ingredients that are essential to actualization:

Intention + Willpower + Resource → Actualization

Let's take a closer look at these ingredients and examine how they combine to make things happen for us:

- **Ingredient 1: Intention:** To see an idea, ambition, or dream through to fruition, you must have a clear vision of what it is you wish to actualize. An *intention* is a blueprint for whatever it is that you wish to create or bring about. Perhaps you want to lose twenty pounds, or improve a relationship, or create a business. The more focused your intention, the more quickly and effectively it can be accomplished. The exercises for this chapter offer a detailed tutorial for crafting clear and focused intentions.

- **Ingredient 2: Willpower** Chapter 1 explored the idea that *energy* is the underlying substance of all things. To actualize an intention is to infuse it with energy, to give it real substance. You do this by focusing attention on it, taking willful action to see it through, and reflecting on your progress regularly. All the while you imbue the intention with personal power. You invest your vital energy to *fulfill* it—to make it happen. The more grand or expansive an intention is, the more energy it requires. For example, it takes far more energy to grow a redwood tree than it takes to grow a daisy. The Art of Empowerment (Chapter 1) enables you to build your willpower in order to fulfill your intentions.

- **Ingredient 3: Resource** It is possible to bring about personal improvement through intentions and willpower alone, but most ambitions require additional resources. Some require *physical resources* such as materials, supplies, equipment, media, and facilities. Others require *intellectual resources* such as information, education, and communication tools. Most require *human resources* such as networks, partnerships, services, and support. To effectively make big things happen, you must know how to access the abundance of resources available in society. Given that society is inherently *social*, you tap into this abundance by building relationships, collaborating and communicating effectively, developing inter-reliant partnerships, and investing in the success of others.

To make most things happen all three of these ingredients must be combined. For example, if your intention is *unclear* or *poorly devised*, the greatest willpower and resource available will quickly actualize something *unclear* and *poorly devised*. Alternatively, you may have an excellent intention, but without the willpower to effectively see it through it will float around as a pie-in-the-sky fantasy that never comes to fruition. Say you have both the intention and the will, but you assemble inadequate resources or an under-qualified team. If so, your ambition is likely to fall apart over time, never fully piecing together as a success.

The best advice that anyone ever gave me is this: "Buy the best; cry once." The lesson that I took from it was that it is best to *fully invest yourself in all that you do*. Take the hurt up-front, and then reap the rewards from that moment on. Take time to carefully craft your intention. Gather the will necessary to see it through. Proceed with high quality resources and, if appropriate, with a team of experts who fill specifically identified needs. Infuse your ambition with excellence each step of the way. It will cost you up front, but once it is truly actualized you will reap the rewards forever-after.

The day I graduated from college a close friend of mine and I walked along the beach for hours pondering the rest of our lives. "I'm going to build a different kind of school some day," I had declared, feeling utterly exhausted by my own education. "It will be a place that wakes kids up to the magic of learning rather than burning them out. Year after year they'll feel like they can't wait for summer to be over so they can get back to school. The program won't just target academic excellence, but a balance of physical, social, emotional, creative and civic development as well. Kids will awaken the *holistic excellence* in themselves and then put it to use."

Ten years after setting this intention I found myself welcoming kindergarten through sixth grade students to their very first day at a brand new public charter school, one that I had founded with a business partner. The previous decade had been spent researching both educational theory and the process of school development. Much of that time I had apprenticed under a master educator, helping her to found a private school.

Upon opening this new public school, I had a very focused intention and an abundance of will. However, I grossly underestimated the importance of the third ingredient of actualization, which is *resource*. As the project unfolded, I nearly lost everything—my life included—by neglecting it.

In our first couple years, despite the ups and downs of opening a major business, we had everything going for us. My codirector was a brilliant and dynamic business woman, equally impassioned about our mission. We had a dedicated staff and tremendously supportive families. We were quite a success by the end of our second year and most of our clientele were delighted.

Yet it became increasingly apparent that my personal approach to management was overly self-centered. I did not incorporate other resources adequately into the process. Working to cut costs, I filled too many roles and responsibilities, and I spent much time reinventing the wheel rather than accessing useful resources or services that were abundantly available. As the years passed I felt increasingly overburdened. My energy steadily declined, along with my effectiveness and my health.

The turning point came in our fifth year as we faced the prospect of having to close the school. I was dealing with life-threatening ailments. In this critical hour I had to abandon my post. When I did, a very interesting thing happened. The school kept functioning without me. In fact, the entire community came together more committed to our mission than ever before. Roles and responsibilities were quickly reorganized, all for the betterment of the school. One of our former teacher/administrators rose to become a visionary principal.

In the seven months that it took to regain my strength and health, I looked long and hard at my failures and at the effects that they had on hundreds of other people. I came to recognize the true importance of *resource* in the process of actualizing an ambition.

Committed as ever to our mission, I returned to the program in a new role—one that I was better suited to fulfill. I set out to create a governance structure that would capitalize on the immense resources available to us within the community, to develop a powerful board of directors that would oversee the organization, and to spearhead the collaborative development of a strategic plan in order to ensure the fulfillment of our mission.

Some twenty years after walking along the beach, imagining grand possibilities, the school that I had dreamed of was honored with the award for *Best Charter School of the Year* in our state—recognized for our innovative mission, our academic accomplishments, and our unique approach to involving community members and resources in our governance. This achievement was made possible by the collaboration of an entire community, of which I was but one, small part. As a joyous aside, I commonly heard from parents that their children couldn't wait for summer to end each year so that they could get back to school.

In this truly humbling process, I learned the following essential lessons about the art of actualization:

- Actualization requires a balance of three ingredients—*intention, willpower,* and *resource.* Neglect any one of these ingredients and we inhibit our success. The next chapter will focus on different aspects of how to access *resources.*

- Regardless of who sets the initial intention, key roles and responsibilities must be identified, and partners must take the roles best suited for their areas of expertise.

- Actualization is a process. It has ups and downs. By deeply and honestly examining both *successes* and *failures* along the way, we learn from them. These lessons allow us to improve on our processes, and to move step-by-step forward toward fulfillment.

- Persistence is essential to actualization. The Art of Empowerment (Chapter 1) enables us to gather and maintain the strength of will necessary to see things through to fruition.

We each have the power to effect tremendous creativity and change in our lives, generally far more than we realize. The art of actualization enables us to overcome adversity, heal illnesses, cultivate success, nourish relationships, and will our own grand designs into being. It allows us to be purposeful in what we use our energies to create. Most importantly, it awakens the artist in each of us and makes life itself a work of art.

Chapter 7 Exercises

Exercise 7a: The Art of Setting Intentions

We tend to hold many intentions at the same time, only some of which we consciously recognize. As a result, our various intentions often conflict or compete with one another, inhibiting the fulfillment of any given one. To be effective in the art of actualization it is important to identify the spread of intentions that you hold in order to avoid working against yourself. This exercise will help you identify your major intentions, explore how each of the five categories function within you, and offer specific tools for managing them.

Begin by reading through the five forms of intention listed on pages 124-127. Then read through the story that follows on page 127. Try to identify each form of intention as it arises in Rose's story, then in June's story. *How do these various intentions operate? What outcomes do they affect?*

Think about some of the intentions that are active in your own life. Make a list of the major long-term goals, ambitions, dreams or accomplishments that you hope to achieve. Create a second list of the more immediate goals and objectives you hold, things that you hope to accomplish in the next week or month. In both these lists, consider a range of goals, including personal, social, work-related, creative, financial, health and wellness oriented, spiritual, etc.

You are now going to organize these various intentions. Using a notepad or word processing document, create a new page for each of the five categories: *micro-intentions, strategic intentions, macro-intentions, curricular intentions and existential intentions.* As you read through the descriptions of each type below, think back over the various goals that you wrote down on your short-term and long-term lists. Try to identify which category each of your goals belongs to, and copy it onto that specific page. A goal to run a marathon may make it onto your *strategic intention* page, while a goal to clean the garage might land on your *micro-intention* page. A goal to improve your eating habits can be addressed as a *strategic intention* or a *macro-intention,* depending on the approach you wish to take. If you're not sure, just guess.

Read through the following descriptions to better understand the nature of each category, and to organize your various goals accordingly:

Micro-Intentions—These are the specific intentions that drive your basic, individual activities. Common examples include *practicing a skill, doing an assignment or chore, taking a shower, getting together with a friend, going to an appointment, preparing dinner, exercising, criticizing someone, and so on.* Some of them are conscious; others are directed automatically by mental programming. Thoughts play a significant role in setting this form of intention. Every thought you have acts as a kind of micro-intention, whether it is productive or destructive. By choosing which thoughts to have and which to avoid, you gain greater control over what you create for yourself. The Art of Focus (Chapter 3) and the Art of Mindfulness (Chapter 4) enable you to command the various thoughts and mental programs that drive your micro-intentions each day.

Strategic Intentions—Major goals, dreams, ambitions and pursuits are powerfully actualized through strategic intentions. By nature, this form of intention is practical, linear, logical, organized, efficient, systematic and left-brained in its approach. It can be used to fulfill *health goals, educational goals, career and business goals, or to tackle major assignments, improve relationships, increase productivity, develop skills and talents, etc.* Strategic intentions focus and coordinate your efforts. They can engender tremendous personal growth, and are even more valuable to organizations, groups and teams. Exercise 7b will offer a detailed tutorial for developing strategic intentions.

Macro-Intentions—While strategic intentions are methodical, macro-intentions are more mystical. By nature the macro-intention is intuitive, fluid, artful, meditative, holistic, and right-brained in its approach. It requires tremendous willpower to be successfully fulfilled. Much like prayer, it supports initiatives and aspirations such as *improving health or well-being, altering a lifestyle, changing an attitude, deepening intimacy, increasing authenticity, developing a quality, attribute or personality trait, and so on.* The key is to develop a simple and clear intention and then to affirm that intention frequently in the present tense, as if it is already true. "I am a good listener," for example. Use your right forefinger to press the center of your left palm as you say the words in your mind. Think of this as a biological button that activates the intention, or as a physiological prayer. Imagine the energy of your intention radiating from every fiber of your being. When facing a related challenge or decision, activate your macro-intention by stating it in your mind and pressing that physiological button in your left palm. *Intuition* will automatically come to mind instructing you on how best to proceed. Realize however that you might not like what it has to say. It may instruct you to "stop blabbering and ask her a thoughtful question," for example. If you lack the willpower to follow the intuitions that arise, the Art of Empowerment (Chapter 1) can help you gather the strength you need. Alternatively, try using a strategic intention instead. The following chapter on *presence* will offer further support for successfully fulfilling macro-intentions.

Curricular Intentions—These are primarily the subconscious intentions that drive your ongoing growth from one developmental stage to the next. Many operate without your awareness of them. As a result, they can frequently conflict with other more conscious intentions that you hold. The Art of Cultivation (Chapter 5) enables you to recognize and address this form of intention. Through the process, you learn to fulfill your curricular intentions so that they do not conflict with your other, more conscious intentions or aspirations. The exercises in Chapter 5 support you in doing this.

Existential Intentions—Embedded in the deepest layers of consciousness, existential intentions drive you to fulfill a unique sense of character, life-mission, or purpose. They give rise to many of your lifelong curricular intentions and to your unique passions and interests. They can guide many of the other forms of intention from behind the scenes. Chapter 8: The Art of Presence will explore this form of intention in greater detail, and will offer specific techniques for unearthing and supporting it. It will help you to align all your various other forms of intention around these deepest expressions of self.

If you have not already done so, take time to organize the various short-term and long-term intentions that you identified earlier into these five categories. Your basic goals are mostly *micro-intentions*. Your major ambitions and pursuits are mostly *strategic or macro-intentions*. While it is valuable to be aware of *curricular* and *existential intentions*, this tutorial emphasizes how to focus your conscious energy on fulfilling the first three forms.

All intentions require *energy* in order to be fulfilled. If you hold too many intentions, you are likely to watch them all fizzle. New *micro-intentions* arise hour after hour and can easily overrun each day. If you wish to address bigger intentions, you will have to *prioritize* these bigger intentions into your lifestyle. Clear a half-hour or full hour daily to get your momentum going. If this seems impractical or unattainable, it is important to realize that tough decisions must sometimes be made when setting priorities in your life. *Which of your activities are essential? Which are merely habitual?*

It is possible to run several major intentions simultaneously, but you must take the time to set each one up for success. Study the intentions that you listed in the *strategic* and *macro-intention* categories. Pick the one, single intention that is most important to you. Does it conflict with your *curricular* or *existential intentions? Is it in alignment with them?* Be aware of the challenges that you may face in seeing this intention through.

You are going to give this one intention everything you've got until it's off the ground and running. If it is a *macro-intention*, study the macro-intention descriptions on pages 125 and 135. The active reflection technique on page 38 can help you proceed in accomplishing it. The following chapter will offer more tools to support the process. The key with a *macro-intention* is to affirm it frequently each day. Surround yourself with creative reminders of it. Ask others to hold your success in their thoughts. This will increase the amount of willpower directed through it.

If you have chosen a strategic intention, proceed to Exercise 7b.

Once your first major intention is launched, you may begin to get another one going—if, and only if, you have the time and energy to tackle both simultaneously. Consider assigning each one to specific days of the week or alternating weeks. This insures that both will progress.

Exercise 7b: Fulfilling Strategic Intentions

Strategizing is a valuable life skill used to focus and direct personal power aptly and potently toward major objectives. It breaks a seemingly insurmountable ambition down into smaller, attainable steps. It organizes activities in order to insure maximum accomplishment with minimal effort. To strategically actualize an intention, take the following steps:

STEP 1: MISSION

The heart of a strategic intention is its mission. *What is it that you are intent on accomplishing? In the case of creating an organization, for example, what is it that you will do or provide?* Every strategic action will be driven by your mission statement, so this statement should be as clear, brief, positive, and specific as possible. To begin, list the important elements of your mission in keywords or phrases: *lose 30 pounds, healthy, attractive, get in shape, not eat bad food, not starve myself.* Change negative statements to positive ones: *eat healthy food, feel energized and well nourished.* Now put these ideas together into a sentence: *I intend to get in shape, lose 30 pounds, and be attractive, healthy, energized and well nourished.* Whittle away at it until it is focused and clear. Get down to the bare-bones: *it is my mission to be healthy, fit and attractive.* If you are developing a team mission with partners, every individual must feel personal ownership and inspiration when reading the mission statement. This process can be very valuable for nourishing intentional growth in a personal relationship or family.

STEP 2: VISION

Where the "mission" is a statement of your intent, the "vision" describes the eventual result or outcome. Start by listing the major elements of what success will look like once your intention is accomplished. Some of the elements that were cut out of your mission may find a place here in the vision. Whittle this new list down into a concise vision statement, just as you had done with the mission. If necessary, you can break it down into different phases. *When phase one is accomplished, my regular lifestyle will include: (1) an enjoyable exercise program, and (2) healthy eating habits that satisfy me while giving my body just the nourishment it needs. When phase two is accomplished, I will have the physique and the attitude of an athlete; my health will be radiant and will inspire others to lead lifestyles that bring out the best in themselves.* A vision statement paints the ideal scenario or endpoint to inspire your efforts along the way. Imagery, drawings, or photos can be useful additions to help you to visualize the goal that you are intent on fulfilling.

STEP 3: CONDITIONS

It is now time to take stock of the forces that will affect your success. Create a chart of all the internal/personal and external/team strengths and weaknesses that will influence your mission. Figure 8 provides an example of this step. Next, consider the obstacles or competitive forces that might get in your way. List them. Don't only consider external factors, but also internal factors such as fears, judgments, emotional issues, attitudes, and types of internal resistance. Next, ask yourself (or your team) this: *Will the current economic or political climate affect the mission either positively or negatively? Who will be affected by our mission, and how might they contribute to or detract from our success? Finally, what support and resources will we need, such as information materials, facilities, people, and time?* This is a very important part of the process. It gives you an overview of everything you have to work with, everything you will need to acquire, and everything that you must overcome in order to fulfill your mission. If working on a team, members should do this exercise individually first and then compare their answers.

STEP 4: MILESTONES

You may now begin planning. Consider the *major* actions and activities that must be accomplished in order to fulfill your mission. Don't worry about the little specific steps just yet. List only the major milestones on your path from beginning to end. Write each one on its own index card or sticky note. Your mission and vision statements (Steps 1 and 2) will help spark ideas. Your various notes on conditions (Step 3) should also fuel the brainstorming process. This is where strategizing comes in. As you develop your milestone cards, lay them out on the floor and begin to order them in a manner that makes the best logical sense to you. You may work from beginning to end, or start with the endpoint—your fully realized vision—and plan backwards from there. Alternatively, you may organize them in a creative design. Some milestones will be grouped together at the same point in time while others will stand alone. Once they are all ordered, walk through them in your imagination to visualize how each step will unfold and lead to the next.

	Internal/Personal	External/Team
Strengths	Highly motivated, history of athletic success, good runner, somewhat flexible	John, Mike and Judy are motivated too; John and Judy have good follow-through
Weaknesses	Tendency toward overwork; skipping meals, overeating late at night; not getting enough sleep; getting down on myself	Our schedules are tight, so it might be hard to coordinate times; Mike can be unreliable
Obstacles and/or Competitive Forces	Funds for proper gear, equipment, gym memberships, high quality food; history of dropout syndrome 3 months in	Fast food advertising and pricing make poor food habits very alluring; winter snow and rain make outdoor exercise difficult; August heat does the same
Climate (Geographic, Social, Economic, Systemic)	I feel better about myself when I'm fit and healthy; my sex life is better when I'm fit and healthy	Local parks and trails are thriving; much ado about health consciousness in the media; healthy restaurants and markets on the rise; friends, family and colleagues admire good health
Resources	Willpower; enthusiasm; thoughtful planning; desire to be fit, healthy and attractive; research and preparation; careful budgeting; celebrating successes along the way	Nutritionists, fitness trainers, gyms; good books and internet sites on health and fitness; home delivery meal programs available for breakfast and lunch; teaming up with John, Mike and Judy

Figure 8. *Example of a "Conditions" Chart*

Did you miss any key steps? Are there problems with your order of events? When you feel confident about the general path, give each step a target date of completion. You now have a strategic timeline guiding you from step one to the actualization of your mission. Example: *get expert advice from a nutritionist, trainer, therapist, etc. by completion date February 1; start a blog on my life-transformation experience February 1; set things up with John, Mike and Judy February 1; explore various types of food and exercise February 1; exercise and eat healthy 3x/week March 1; pick a primary sport March 1; train and eat healthy 4x/week April 1; 20 pounds lighter May 1; cross-train and eat healthy 5x/week May 1; join a team or league June 15; 30 pounds lighter in peak condition July 15; athlete's attitude, presence and lifestyle July 15; Hawaii celebration August 1.*

STEP 5: ACTIONS

This is where you get down to business. Take a look at the first milestone on your timeline or the first group of milestones if they fall together in roughly the same place. Create a step-by-step checklist of each individual task or action item that must be accomplished in order to fulfill this milestone. Note any resources or support that will be needed to see it through to fruition. If you are working with a team, assign each task to a well-qualified individual who will be accountable for it.

Set a target completion date. These deadlines are not meant to create a sense of fear or oppression, but simply to keep things on track and catalyze optimal efforts. If this is a personal mission, set your target dates of completion for each task and try to schedule work-times for the first few. You have now created an "Action Plan." Take one minute to look over your tasks every morning to keep them in the forefront of your awareness. As you complete each one, check it off on your list. If appropriate, consider photo-journaling the process to build excitement. Honor each accomplishment—no matter how small—with a little personal celebration, perhaps a smile, a thumbs-up, or an imagined pat on the back. Once a *milestone* is accomplished, create an Action Plan for the next one or ones. To increase efficiency, create an action plan for "milestone b" before you complete "milestone a," giving yourself time to prepare for it and gather resources. An Internet search on creating a "Gantt Chart" will offer other valuable tools. It will help you to map out your milestones and action steps within a specific time frame.

STEP 6: REFLECTIONS

A strategic intention is not meant to be cold, rigid, or mechanical. It is meant to be vibrant and inspiring. It is meant to bring out the finest of your capabilities and your humanity. This sixth step is by far the most important, since it keeps the lifeblood of the mission warm, refreshed, and flowing. At the end of each milestone you must reflect on your process and progress. *How do you feel about the mission and vision? Is your strategy maximizing effectiveness while minimizing your expenditure of energy? Do you need to revise your milestones or timeline? Do you need additional resources, or find it necessary to reorganize your team? How do you feel about your efforts and accomplishments? How do you feel about your work with others? What successes and failures have you encountered along the way? What have you learned from them? What will you do differently from now on?* You are not engaged in this mission merely to fulfill it. You are on an ambitious journey to push yourself and grow as a person, to experience meaning and purpose in your life through whatever pursuit you have chosen. Whether you are climbing Mount Everest or learning to walk again after an accident, the real expedition comes in how you elevate yourself as a person each step of the way. Consider tracking your progress regarding various habits, talents, and skills. Be sure to revise and update your strategy from time to time, accounting for unanticipated circumstances or changes in your mission. In this manner you can get from the base to the top of your Everest—whatever that Everest may be—one thoughtful step at a time.

Strategic intentions require ambition and persistence. The process of developing a mission and setting out to see it through reveals many personal strengths and abilities along the way. It can be an inspiring and energizing experience, yet it is important to set yourself up for success. Start with something small to build your skills, confidence, and willpower. Create a simple *strategic intention* that you can accomplish in a month or less. Taste the success.

An attitude of "excellence" will make all the difference when tackling a major ambition. Many people find this word intimidating because it was tarnished through their schooling experiences. Excellence is not about the A+ or perfection. Give the best that you have to give to any one, individual act—no matter how small—and excellence is accomplished. This approach brings about continual self-improvement, and with this comes an ever-increasing mastery of action.

ESSENTIAL QUESTIONS

Take a few moments to ponder the following questions. Allow your-self to come up with at least three answers to each question as a means of self-discovery. Keep a written record of your answers in a log or journal.

- When do I feel most awake and alive?

- What do I spend a majority of my time doing?

- How might I increase my time spent feeling vibrantly alive?

CHAPTER 8

The Art of Presence

No matter where you go, there you are.

—CONFUCIUS, teacher, philosopher and political theorist (551–479 BCE)

Have you ever shared a spontaneous smile with someone and felt surprisingly absorbed by the sudden depth of connection? Have you ever found yourself awed by the beauty of a moment while it unfolded within and around you? Have you ever had an opportunity appear out of thin air with such curiously perfect timing that you couldn't help but wonder, *Is this really just a coincidence?*

What does it truly mean "to be in the right place at the right time"? Do luck, fortune, or privilege deliver us there, or are they simply among the gifts that can be found once we have arrived? What if there is a way to access the seemingly magical moments in life at any time of day or night throughout every week of every year?

Presence is the art of tapping life's abundant possibilities—of opening our eyes to the multitude of gifts that are always right in front of us. It is a heightened state of consciousness that gives rise to our awesome capacity for creativity, and provides direct access to the wealth of potentiality that exists within and around us.

For one who wishes to develop this art, three topics are of value:

1. **The Nature of Imagination**—Exploring your inner window to the vast possibilities that are available to you.

2. **The Art of Storytelling**—Recognizing that much of your life and many of your experiences might be scripted by old and inaccurate stories that you tell about yourself and your potential.

3. **Living in a State of Presence**—Learning to direct your creativity toward the plentiful possibilities that call to be realized within and around you.

The Nature of Imagination

Who would have thought that a mother might one day be able to give her own kidney to an ailing son in order to save his life? *Someone* must have had this thought.

Who would dream that a man could leave this planet and step foot on the moon? *Someone* must have held this dream.

Who would imagine that people across the globe might someday instantly communicate with one another? *Someone*, or *some group of individuals,* obviously dared to do so.

Imagination is one of our greatest human capacities. It allows us to envision things that exist beyond the realm of what we hold as possible, and then to astonish ourselves by actualizing those impossibilities. Like magic, imagination heals terminal illness, turns science fiction into working technology, and inspires or even transforms civilizations.

It is commonly believed that some of us *are* imaginative while others *are not*. This is much like believing that some of us have lungs while others do not. Though we may be unable to see these and various other internal organs, they continually operate inside us just the same. Take away our lungs, or take away our imagination, and the show is instantly over.

Anything that we create—a meal, an appointment, a thought, an opinion, an opportunity, a work of art, a mistake—requires imagination. To plan ahead, to consider that which has not yet happened, you are by definition *imagining*. To reconsider something that has already happened, you are doing the same; you are imagining a new telling of an old story. In reading these words and deriving any kind of meaning from them, you are coauthoring this book through your imagination as you bring your own insights to these words. All perception, all creativity, all free thought, all enterprise, and all conscious growth are driven by imagination.

In early childhood we instinctively give ourselves over to imagination, enabling tremendous growth and development. For example, we *imagine* moving about independently, and then will ourselves into motion by rolling, crawling, and sitting up. We soon imagine standing like those we see around us, and drive ourselves against the force of gravity to eventual success. We form hopes and dreams and imagine grand possibilities for ourselves and our world. As painter Vincent Van Gogh once put it, "I dream my painting, and then I paint my dream."

In youth we often look to others for the inspiration to imagine, to dream, and to develop ambitions. Similarly, we look to them to see how these things are actualized. If those around us resist creativity, discredit imagination, and allow a fear of failure to inhibit them, we tend to follow in their footsteps. We too grow fearful of possibilities *too grand* or the risks associated with them. We learn to lower our sights to more "reasonable" aims, no matter how limited and arbitrary that sense of reasonableness may be. We become practical. Our lives become safe, comfortable, and mundane.

All the while, the spirit of imagination shines brightly inside us. Our personal power calls to reach far and wide, to radiate freely like starlight. By suppressing this natural expression of will, a critical fracture takes place deep inside us. We learn quite ironically to *pretend* that we are not imaginative, concealing this inherent capacity like an embarrassing secret. In the act of concealment, we imprison the heart of our creative power.

A sense of yearning may soon follow, arising as our hopes and dreams cry out from deep within the imagination to protest their divorce from our actual, everyday lives. Art, music, film, and various other media provide temporary relief, elevating us out of the ruts that we dig and the limits that we set for ourselves. We find ourselves temporarily returned to the imaginative realm of possibility that is the eternal playground of human consciousness. Seeing things if only momentarily from this vibrant vantage point, we sometimes find the inspiration to step out of our habitual limits and re-imagine our lives.

More often than not, however, these moments are more like vacations than real life. Imagination becomes a form of *entertainment*—a passive experience, separate from who we are and what we do. We satisfy it through books, magazines, television, movies, video games, the internet, and spectator sports. Quiet and comfortable in our *living rooms*, we observe the extraordinary lives and creativity of others. Our imaginations begin to lead vicarious and voyeuristic lives, and we may soon find ourselves doing the same. Like the recluse who plays out his existence in cyberspace, we can be led astray from tangible and authentic interactions, from challenge and intimacy—from the ultimate sources of human vitality and inspiration.

Imagination is not meant to separate us from *real life*. It is meant to help us access the highest level of what is possible for ourselves and others in our real, everyday lives. Exercise 8a offers various techniques for reengaging the imagination in a healthy manner, employing its immense creative power to improve the quality of our actual lives.

The Art of Storytelling

One beautiful summer in Southern California, six close friends and I decided to spend a week together on a kind of "revitalization" retreat. We were each at a transition point in life, facing upcoming shifts in our schooling, careers, relationships, and families. We came together to wipe our slates clean of old habits and attitudes and to embrace the new era of opportunities that lay before us.

On our first night together, one among us gashed his finger while preparing dinner. He stood there at the kitchen sink watching his blood flow into the drain, and slowly drifted into shock. This catalyzed a chain of events that drew each of us completely into the present moment, quite effectively wiping our slates clean. We couldn't help but notice the curious timing of this event.

The next day, still struck by the power of the experience, we all went to a café and reflected on the strange night that we had shared. One by one, each of us offered his or her unique perspective on what had happened. We began with the story of the person least involved, and worked our way through to the climactic accounting of our friend who had actually gashed himself.

Each telling was surprisingly different, so much so that some hardly seemed to describe the same experience. Interestingly, each story was also strikingly similar to the particular storyteller's personality and outlook on life. This led us to wonder. *To what extent are our stories a product of actual events? To what extent are they a product of our personalities?*

If you think about it, any story told includes only a minute fraction of the details from the actual experience it describes. We pick through the details in our memories and share only those aspects that are relevant to the points we wish to make, to the feelings we hope to relate, to the connections we seek to develop, to the beliefs and attitudes that we hold, or to the things that we are working to better understand.

Sitting there in the café with my friends, I watched as we turned a real experience into a series of highly subjective stories that seemed less about the event and more about the players. I wondered what effect these stories might have on each of us, subtle or great.

A random inventory of my own stories flashed through my awareness—the ones that I most commonly told about myself and my life. There were clear themes and patterns among them. I began to get the haunting impression that regardless of how skewed or subjective these stories were, they did not simply recount my past, but actually influenced how my future was unfolding.

Chapter 3 on The Art of Focus explored the idea that attention directs our energy. It asserted that whatever we focus on tends to grow and expand. In this manner the stories that we tell about ourselves, our relationships, and our lives act as *the sixth form of intention*. They don't merely describe the past. They focus our energies on very specific aspects of that past. They feed and therefore perpetuate those specific aspects into the future. In other words, the stories you tell about your past and present tend to directly influence the script of your future.

Upon examining some of my common stories—many of which did not describe the person I was intent on becoming—I decided to re-explore my history, looking for evidence of powerful moments that life had offered me. By telling this new set of stories, I drew that power into my present and let it spill over into my future. It was like performing magic. My life began to reflect the positivity, optimism, and prosperity that this new set of "true" stories recounted.

Consider the case of a woman mugged and then left for dead in an alley. Her *tragedy* is the most gripping and newsworthy part of her story, so it is the content that is aired on prime time television and radio.

Now consider the homeless man who ran to the woman's aid, and the paramedics who got her to the hospital in under twelve minutes, and the numerous vehicles that pulled over to play their part, and the nurses, technicians, doctors, administrators, custodians, donors, insurance partners, city systems, taxpayers, and all the countless other forces that conspired to keep her alive and present on Earth.

Which of these stories will the woman choose to tell—the myopic, newscast version of her victimization, or that bigger-picture version of society's abundant gesture with her in a moment of need? Which door to the future will she choose to open for herself?

When telling the story of your life, it is of great value to recognize and focus on the details that reveal or inspire an empowered unfolding of your being. Much like rewriting your own DNA, every aspect of your life and growth will emanate from the building blocks of your history—however you choose to tell it. This is not to suggest that you should deny or bury your mistakes, traumas or misfortunes, but rather, recognize and reveal them within an empowered context of a bigger picture.

Consider a few common statements that people make—subtle stories or myths that they tell about their lives and circumstances. Think about the influence that each of these stories might have on the teller's future:

I am underprivileged.

My parents really screwed me up.

Only when I'm completely exhausted and overwhelmed do I know that I'm working hard enough.

Nobody understands me.

Nobody really loves me.

I'm a terrible person, unredeemable.

I *used to be* really good at …

The art of storytelling is not about being dishonest with ourselves or others or weaving fictional yarns. Rather, it's about weeding through our endless life-details to author and then propagate empowering descriptions of where we've been, who we are, and what we intend to become.

Not only does *the spin* on a story shape our future; *the seriousness* with which we tell that story affects the future as well. We tend to forget that stories are, after all, just stories. They are long strings of words and memories—pure abstractions. They hold no direct, concrete connection to the multifaceted nature of real experiences that we have or to the real and unscripted beings that we are in each present moment.

When we learn to step outside that seriousness and attachment to our stories, outside the tales that we tell about the nature of people and things, we provide open space in our lives where nothing is certain, and therefore new possibilities are free to emerge. This *uncertainty* is like a fertile field that allows us to imaginatively seed our own futures, to create and then fulfill our freshest and most vibrant designs for the unfolding of our lives.

There is an art to awakening this powerful creativity—stepping outside our thoughts and words into the realm of action. We are all born as masters of this art, *Presence*, yet we tend to lose sight of it during the course of a modern upbringing. Nonetheless, it is an art that is always available within, always there to be rediscovered.

Living in a State of Presence

The present moment is the leading edge of life. It is that place where all conscious action occurs, where all intentions are set, where all creativity unfolds, and where all possibilities are actualized. We are often so caught up in our minds that we miss much of what goes on right here, right now. We drift off, thinking about past moments, or future ones. We concern ourselves with how things should be going rather than involving ourselves in how they actually are going. All the while the present moment slips by as an under used, under-appreciated resource. In turn, our capacity to creatively affect our own lives is diminished.

We have a limited number of minutes here on earth and an unfathomable degree of freedom in how we spend them. As the clock ticks away, opportunities hang in the air around us like fruits waiting to be plucked. By learning to reach into the moment at hand and notice these opportunities, we enable ourselves to actualize a bounty of life possibilities.

Presence is a heightened state of consciousness available to anyone in any walk of life. There are several common activities that notoriously distract us from it:

Internal Dialogue

As we develop language skills we also develop an endless stream of thought inside our heads. We incessantly describe the world to ourselves, and describe ourselves to ourselves. We tell stories about things that have happened, things that might happen, or things that we want to have happen, all the while missing much of what is actually happening. By learning to quiet this mental noise, one's attention can be turned to the many things happening here and now.

Chatter

Just as we tend to blabber on and on inside our heads, we also feel the need to fill time with others through endless talk about everything under the sun. If and when we run out of fresh things to say, we start recycling old thoughts, telling stories of yore, or just making stuff up to fill time. This chatter becomes a substitute for action and exploration, siphoning attention away from the vital possibilities available at present.

Agendas

We commonly develop fixed ideas about how things are supposed to happen, when and why they should happen, how people are supposed to behave, and even who we expect people to be—ourselves included. When things go differently than expected, we may resist or fight them, often missing out on opportunities that are only temporarily accessible to us.

Destinations

Poets may suggest that the journey is the thing, but for most of us the goal or the destination is what we seek. We can quickly plummet into the depths of struggle when our journeys stray from their desired ends. Anxious to complete the work, to move onto the next thing, or to get where we want to be, we leap from one task to the next, missing much of what is abundantly available in the space between. By learning to suspend the mental activities that siphon away our attention, we free up awareness and energy for the moment at hand. In doing this, we often find that we are actually five steps closer to everything that we want or need. We find ourselves surrounded by abundant possibilities that were formerly obscured by the mental noise inside.

The average young adult tends to get caught up like the rest of us in the shuffle of a busy life, relinquishing the spontaneity and enthusiasm of youth. We write this off as a part of maturation, yet deep inside we may occasionally question whether something important has been lost. That vitality, those beaming smiles, that sense of abandoning yourself to the moment—these qualities are not unique to childhood. *They are not meant to be outgrown.* Once lost, we inevitably feel an occasional yearning to reclaim them.

For most of us this yearning begins before we graduate high school. Subconscious though it may be, we look for ways to disengage ourselves from the relentless flow of internal dialogue and chatter, and from the multitude of agendas and destinations that bind our activities. By temporarily freeing our attention from these things, we free all the corresponding personal power directed by that attention. The experience feels awakening and invigorating.

Drugs and alcohol are commonly used to catalyze this process. By disrupting our common mental activities, they allow us to attend more fully to the present moment. Almost magically, the door to *now* is reopened. Unable to access a state of presence independently, however, we quickly become dependent upon these substances to access it for us. Before long we find ourselves having to up the dosage to maintain the experience. This dependency can create a consuming mental agenda known as an addiction, drawing us even further away from our inherent state of presence.

Many of us learn to use healthier vehicles such as arts, sports, hobbies, and vacations to catalyze that sense of presence, yet these are often fairly focused activities in-and-of themselves, directing our attention toward specific ends. Again, many of the abundant opportunities around us go unnoticed.

Young children are naturally masters of presence. Several intrinsic mechanisms allow them to access and maintain this state of being *directly*. These same mechanisms can be used by anyone at any age to reclaim and nourish a state of presence, and therein, to access great possibilities:

[1] OBSERVATION

Much like operating a camera, we have tremendous control over where and how we focus our attention. We can zero in on minute details or widen the field of vision to a panoramic scope. By quietly gazing about with the fascination and rapture of a young child, awareness becomes a window to information and possibilities that otherwise slip by unnoticed. *Observation* is the art of reaching for things by truly noticing them, allowing their splendor to pervade our awareness. *Consider the case of a man in the midst of a midlife crisis. George is dissatisfied with his administrative career at a radio station and finds himself feeling generally unimportant, even at home. A sense of tension has begun to cloud every aspect of his life. Tonight he finds himself at the center of another family argument as he struggles to express his frustration. At the height of exasperation, he cuts himself off mid-sentence and stares blankly at his wife. He notices her long beautiful eyelashes and becomes fascinated by the care with which she has groomed herself. He feels a strange impulse, and spontaneously leans forward to kiss her. As he draws back, he notices the hint of a smile in her soft cheek, and soon feels one forming in his own. "What were we arguing about?" he asks. She leans in and returns the kiss.*

[2] MOMENT ARTISTRY

Our personal power has a natural bent, a tendency to flow in accord with our deepest sense of being or life-purpose. Given absolutely free time—unburdened by agendas or expectations—inner interests and callings emerge that are germane to the unique circumstances at hand. *Moment artistry* is a free-flowing and intuitive experience, temporarily giving ourselves over to the dictates of our innermost sense of being. Exercise 8b will explore this technique in greater detail. *Realizing that his life has grown generally unbalanced, George allows himself a half-hour each evening to be impulsive. He walks in the neighborhood, or sits down at the piano, or meditates, or seduces his wife. With time, his moment artistry begins to reach outside the box of habitual behaviors. He discovers unexpected possibilities in mundane things. For example, an old tape recorder opens the doorway to a radio show lurking deep within him—a quirky news program. Profoundly invigorating, George's nightly half-hour sessions eventually expand into a full hour, and the whole family gets involved. They name it "the magic hour" for the creativity that seems to magically emerge during that time.*

[3] INTUITION

Many of us spend our days following other people's rules, doing other people's work, fulfilling other people's plans. Under such circumstances it is easy to lose touch with the authority of one's own inner voice. *Intuition* is the whisper of conscience, a wisdom arising through unexpected thoughts and feelings. We often forget how to decipher it from the rest of the noise inside our heads. By simply paying attention to our random hunches or sensibilities, we unearth this intuition. One arrives on the heels of another, each often louder than the previous. From our deepest layers of consciousness they reach out to guide us. *One night, while trying to find someone to fill the news slot at the radio station where he works, George has a sudden thought: "Host the segment yourself." He shrugs it off and ponders who he might call when given such late notice. Perhaps he can get someone to phone in the segment. Another random thought pops into his mind. "It's 10:00 Sunday night. Who's gonna care?" A strange sense of giddy excitement arises inside him. "Do it!" He feels suddenly so alive, and decides to go for it. The next morning, he finds himself in the station manager's office being reprimanded for his breach of protocol, but he later learns about scores of listeners who have called in during the morning asking about that "amazing newscaster," wanting to know when they can tune into his next show.*

[4] SIGNALS

The easiest way to experience a sense of being *on purpose* in life is to pay attention to feelings and signals that correspond with your actions. Good fortune, coincidence, synchronicity, simplicity, passion, enthusiasm, and cooperation are *green lights*, emerging when your activities are aligned with the deeper flow of energies within and around you. *Yellow lights* arise through feelings such as apprehension, tension, complexity, resistance or skepticism, alerting you that you may be falling out of alignment with what is best. *Red lights* arise when your actions downright contradict the flow of energies within and around you, emerging as obstacles, accidents, adversity, illness, disconnection or grief. By paying attention to impressions, feelings, and consequences associated with your actions, you learn which way to step in forging your path through life. *After two weeks at the news desk, George is quickly promoted to talk show host. Despite the piles of angry faxes from a certain breed of indignant listeners, he finds opportunities arising all around him—the greatest of which is a sense of calling, a personal mission to infuse the world of news-casting with a novel, positive spin. Each part of this journey feels deeply fulfilling to him—including the awkward time slots in the wee hours, his time spent in a make-shift office in the storage closet, and so on. Simply delighted to be on this meaningful path, a consistent sense of fulfillment drives him from one step to the next, helping him to powerfully actualize the stream of possibilities and opportunities that make themselves available to him.*

[5] MYSTERY

We often think we know "the whole story" about the world, or about the people and things in our lives, or even about ourselves. No matter how wise or smart we become, this knowledge only scratches the surface of the true nature of things. By elevating our awareness above the stale impressions that we hold about various people and things— opening ourselves to the *mysteries* beyond what we think we know—a wide-eyed fascination takes the reins to our personal power. We soon find ourselves face to face with fascinating beings who were formerly our humdrum friends and family members, or discover vast possibilities previously obscured by our closed and rigid minds. *Bored with the yearly Christmas party at the station, George plays a game with himself. In his mind, he pretends he is new to the station. He approaches coworkers without any preconceptions of who they are. Much to his surprise, he finds that they really aren't the people he thought he knew so well. He establishes intriguing new connections and manages to infuse the party with an off-beat enthusiasm. All the while, he substantially broadens his network of contacts and collaborators. He makes deep connections with people who quickly become intent on helping him succeed and whose ventures he is intent on supporting.*

[6] SURRENDER

A river's flow is dictated by a conspiracy of powerful, natural forces. Whether calm or turbulent, its complex currents always follow the path of least resistance. Learn to give yourself over to the currents present at any given moment, to work with them instead of working to defy them, and you will likely find yourself having the ride of your life. There, deep in the rapids, the path of least resistance is law. Surrendering to forces more powerful than yourself, honoring the currents at play, you maximize your artfulness and effectiveness in the moment and your ultimate survival as well. *Stranded by the side of the road on his way to an important convention for newscasters, George seats himself on a gravel embankment and gazes out at the desert scenery. "Maybe this is where I'm supposed to be right now," he says aloud, as if speaking to the Joshua tree that stands before him. He begins to wonder how long that tree has stood in that very place, despite the harshness of elements year after year. The tree seems to have a subtle message for him. "I'm alive and well," it reveals in thick branches and bright green blades. "Alive and Well." George smiles, recognizing that these words seem to capture the heart of his message in radio. He has long sought a name for his soon-to-be nationally syndicated program. It eludes him no longer.*

The civilized world provides us with a wide range of comforts, resources, and opportunities, yet civilized life itself can be somewhat over-programmed and restrictive. We often miss out on many of the gifts that we have painstakingly worked to provide for ourselves. The more we tap into our inherent state of presence, however, the more we enable ourselves to truly reap what we have sown.

Nature has a particularly powerful tendency to ignite that sense of presence within. We sometimes experience this phenomenon when spending time in our neighborhood parks. These natural, open environments have a way of drawing you in off the boulevard. Caught in the allure, you may unexpectedly step onto the grass, feeling the pull of something elemental. "Just a quick visit," you tell the kids as they dart off toward the trees. You follow after them, tucking away the shopping list and cellular phone.

Gripped by the smell of rich soil, fresh water, and foliage, perhaps you notice the gentle breeze blowing through town. You take a deep breath and find the spell of your busyness at once interrupted. The day's agenda temporarily takes its leave, and the day itself emerges fresh and vibrant—unwritten. You begin to notice little things like the warm sunlight falling on your skin, and with them, free time seems to magically appear out of thin air.

In this moment, if you allow yourself to remain present, any possibilities that enter your awareness have instant access to a wellspring of personal power within you. If inspiration strikes, for example, your energy is free to feed it right there on the spot. You may remove an old receipt from your pocket and begin scribbling a poem to yourself. Once fulfilled, your attention is again freed to tap the abundance of a new, unwritten moment.

Presence is a radiant state of awareness—uncluttered by all the noise and activity that otherwise pervades our mundane, everyday experiences of life. Most of us spend our early youth mastering this art, only to lose touch with it in adolescence. From time to time, presence will come knocking at the door, inviting itself back into our lives—if only we heed its call. This may arise through a powerful experience such as a journey, relationship, illness or disaster.

My own rediscovery of presence took place during my final year in college. I decided to board with a family in order to keep my expenses down. Mili and I hit it off instantly during our first contact. She was the matriarch of the family, recently divorced. I was aware that she had two kids but figured that they weren't likely to cramp my style. After all, I'd hardly ever be home. If I wasn't at school or out socializing, I'd be in the graduate music studio recording a rock album. All I needed was a bed for an occasional bit of sleep before heading back out into my busy life.

It turns out that the boys—Jake, age 8 and Walt, age 6—had a different vision of how things might unfold between us. One night their mom stayed up late on the off-chance that she would catch me dropping by for a quick sleep. She let me know that the guys were very curious about this new college kid who lived in their home. That very morning before school she had found them peering in through my window to watch me sleep.

I explained that I was quite busy, and that I didn't really have time to hang out with kids. Shortly thereafter, I began to find little notes slipped under my door—pictures that the boys had drawn, or questions they had written in all capital letters like, "DO YOU PLAY BASEBALL?"

It was mildly annoying and yet somewhat charming at the same time. I decided to leave quickly scribbled notes for them in return—messages like, "baseball is alright, but football is better." Eventually cookies and cupcakes started showing up outside my door, and then there appeared an invitation to dinner on Sunday night.

Through an interesting coincidence, I had just discovered that my time slot in the recording studio that Sunday had been cancelled. The vocal booth was to be refurbished. This, combined with a nagging sense of selfishness about avoiding the kids, inspired me to accept their invitation and meet them for dinner.

I would later find out that they spent the entire day preparing the meal. I arrived around four o'clock, after hours of football in the park with my buddies. Standing just outside the front door, I heard a scrambling sound inside, and loud whispers to the effect of, "He's here!" Exhausted and sunburned, I wasn't really in the mood for hanging out with two little punks. Then again, I wasn't about to back out on them now.

I opened the door and stepped inside just in time to watch ankles and feet disappear behind the couch as the boys dove out of sight. There was quite a sense of nervous excitement in the air. They giggled and squirmed about back there behind the couch.

"I can hear you," I said in a goofy tone of voice that surprised me. "Gee, I wonder where you are…"

This inspired a round of mischievous giggles and a scrambling about of knees and elbows against the hardwood floor.

"Is that a foot I see there?" I asked, spying one at the edge of the couch. It quickly disappeared.

Mili was busying herself in the kitchen, trying to stay out of the way. I tiptoed to the couch and peered over the edge. The next thing I knew, I was lying flat on my back, pinned to the floor beneath a tangle of arms and legs. I grabbed the guys by their waists, one in each arm, and struggled to my feet, hoisting them up over my shoulders. They roared and hollered, absolutely delighted to be my captives.

The hours that followed flew by as we played ball in the yard, hide and seek, and so on. We had an animated discussion over dinner, which mostly involved me answering a slew of their various questions about everything under the sun. Before I knew it, Mili was announcing that it was bedtime—for the fourth and final time. I stood and gazed down at Jake and Walt, filled to the brim with an abundant sense of joy. "You guys are awesome," I said, feeling completely energized. "We should do this again next Sunday."

Their faces lit up. They gazed at one another, then back to me.

"All right, then," I said. "Next Sunday it is." I turned away.

"Wait!" Walt hollered. He stood up and took a step toward me, but hesitated.

"What's up, kid?" I asked.

He took another step forward. "I was just wondering…" he said.

"Oh yeah?" I stared at him, curious about what he had to say. He seemed a bit nervous. "What are you wondering about?" I said, trying to coax it out of him.

"Are you the hugging kind?" he asked, his face rosy with the forming of a sheepish smile.

At that very moment, it occurred to me that they'd been picking away at me for months, slowly chipping at the invincibility of my rigid and overscheduled life. All the while I had seen myself as someone too important to waste his time with two little punks who by their very childishness would have little of value to offer a brilliant and mature guy such as myself. Just then, however, I didn't feel so brilliant, or mature either.

"The hugging kind, huh?" I said. It seemed poetic, adorable, and somewhat profound at the same time. *Sure*, I thought. *I'm a member of the hugging kind.* Given that I was wearing a tie-dyed tee shirt garnished with a big peace symbol, this probably didn't seem like a major stretch.

I'm not certain if that's what it was that gave me away, but Walt and Jake scurried forth and wrapped their arms around me. I knelt down to give them a more proper hug and felt reminded of something important. It had been a truly rejuvenating evening, following the tides of unscripted and enthusiastic free play. A sense of spiritedness turned the entire experience—even dish duty and cleanup time—into an exciting and creative affair.

In the days that followed, I focused intently on keeping that spiritedness alive within me. I brought it with me to my classes, to the recording studio, to my late nights in the library, to my various social engagements, and even to the mundane time in between—driving, brushing my teeth, and so on. I realized that for many years, I had confined my conception of creativity to music, forgetting that every aspect of life had room for creative expression. Learning to see the world through a child's eyes once again, I was reminded that time is always better spent when you're fully present in what you are doing—playful, artful, and enthusiastic.

The bigger-picture story that I tell about my first exchange with Walt and Jake is that it drew my awareness to the educator and human development theorist lurking deep within me. I still find it fascinating that the very experience I had resisted and avoided for months was the one that ultimately awakened a sense of life-purpose within me, sending me down a path that has led to the creation of schools, the development/publication of this book, and the formation of organizations that support *human capacities* development.

Many of us learn to reach for fulfillment by trying to control everything in our lives. If and when we open ourselves to the magic of what is truly here, of what calls to be realized in each and every moment, fulfillment reveals itself as an altogether different affair. You don't reach for it, or control it; you acquiesce to it, serving as a vehicle for its unfoldment.

Presence awakens us to the offerings that loom just beyond our plans, beliefs, and expectations. It drives us to lend ourselves with deep satisfaction to that greater exchange of energies in flow all around us. In this heightened state of consciousness, all time emerges as free time, spent like the surfer at dawn who streams half naked, fully awakened, along waves of possibility into the day.

Chapter 8 Exercises

Exercise 8a: The Art of Imagination

Imagination is a capacity for recognizing the possibilities that are available to us, and for drawing those possibilities into our real, everyday lives. Six techniques allow us to make use of it with great effectiveness. These same techniques can be used to reacquaint people with this inherent aspect of their being—even those people who feel unimaginative or skeptical.

Begin this exercise by rereading "The Nature of Imagination" on page 146. Examine the following techniques and choose the one that most resonates with you. The active reflection steps outlined on page 38 will help you develop your chosen technique. Spend at least a week working on it, then consider exploring a different technique the following week.

Asking *"What If?"*
What if our lives are filled with endless possibilities, but our fears and rigid beliefs keep us from considering a vast majority of those possibilities? What if close-mindedness is like a chain that tethers us to one tiny plot on the field of what could be? What if we can unshackle ourselves by asking a simple question? *What if?* This magical question invites us to temporarily suspend our disbelief without actually putting ourselves in harm's way or committing to anything. It opens our eyes to a wider field of possibilities than we might ordinarily consider. To use this technique, ask yourself a *what if* question, and then see where it sends your imagination. *What if I am actually … What if I could… What if I had… What if we were able to … What if …* This question is the basic element of genius, freeing the consciousness to roam about in the expansiveness of pure potential. It provides inspiration for how we might creatively shape ourselves, our relationships, our lifestyles, our

careers, our surroundings, and so on. Once answers and ideas begin to emerge, you can then decide whether or not you wish to pursue them.

Pretending

Author Kurt Vonnegut, Jr. once said, "We are what we pretend to be, so we must be careful about what we pretend to be." Children naturally pretend to be people or various things other than themselves as a means of experiencing new points of view from a first-person perspective. They play in that space for a time, and then they return to the regularity of their ordinary lives. Every one of us has the potential to temporarily explore alternate possibilities of who we are and what we might do with our brief time here on earth. If we pretend long enough, persistently enough, we sometimes find ourselves becoming the very beings that we have pretended to be. Whether we realize it or not, life is a playground in which we constantly redefine ourselves. Take a little time to romp about in the potentiality of who you could be, and you might just find yourself becoming that very person.

Visualization

By picturing something in your mind, imagining it as if it is really happening, you cause your bioenergies to behave in a very specific manner through corresponding thoughts, feelings, and physiological responses. For example, if you feel out of sorts, headachy, ill, or stressed out, visualize yourself seated in the fountain of youth, showered by regenerative and healing waters. See and feel its magical droplets—cool and refreshing—sprinkling gently upon you. Feel them absorbed through your scalp, flowing down through your body and out through your feet into the earth. As they travel through you, picture them physically removing the tension from each of your muscle groups, cleansing you of old distress, freeing you of inhibitions, nourishing the cells throughout your body and immune system. Imagine these droplets infusing you with vibrant health all throughout your being. *By visualizing something in very specific detail, imagining and feeling it through as many independent senses as possible, you cause actual changes to occur in your body, mood, attitude, circumstances, relationships, and so on.* It is not necessary to believe that this phenomenon is possible. Visualization does not require faith. You just have to take the time to do it. Why not give it a try? Give it your best effort, and see what happens.

Practice

We've all had the experience of practicing a skill or talent as a means of improving performance. Perhaps we tossed a ball back and forth a thousand times in order to improve our eye-hand coordination, or ran through scales to familiarize ourselves with the whereabouts of notes on a musical instrument. Just as these concrete forms of practice help us to improve our abilities, *imaginary practice* supports our growth as well. It is also very cost-effective. Simply lie down in a dark room with eyes closed and imagine a state-of-the-art facility for the skill or talent you wish to practice. Imagine the specific equipment that you will use such as a tennis racket or negotiation table. Take a deep breath, and imagine yourself in peak condition—an Olympiad in your field. Imagine engaging in your activity down to very specific details. Feel the perfection in your swing or the compelling nature of your words. Picture the scene in slow motion, and regular motion, and fast motion. Notice the mistakes you make, and correct these mistakes in your imagination. Remember to have fun in the process, to feel a sense of joy, excellence, and effortlessness. This technique promotes tremendous growth in a wide range of activities, including physical rehabilitation. It also develops your capacity for imagination itself. Consider using it just before bed, then setting a dream intention to continue your practice session in sleep. You may amaze yourself with what you soon begin to accomplish.

Art

By engaging in creative forms of self-expression we open a dialog with our innermost dreams, interests and tendencies. Dance, drama, music, film, writing, drawing, painting, sculpting, building sand castles, gardening, cooking, engaging in crafts, and so on, serve as windows to self-awareness. They allow us to practice honestly revealing ourselves through various modalities—light, sound, movement, texture, flavor, shape, and so on—and enable us to access a wider range of the intellectual capacities that are innately available to us. When engaging in art for art's sake, it does not matter how any other person interprets or judges our work. The experience simply invites us to interact with the various media that make up our world and to glimpse at our innermost conscious interests, tendencies, and intuitions.

Personas

Human beings are complex creatures; we tend to bring a lot of baggage with us to our various pursuits. It is possible to simplify ourselves, tailoring our attitudes and identities to meet specific situations and tasks. Imagine a person ideally suited for a particular activity that you face. Consider wearing this *persona* as a means of bringing out specific aspects of yourself, those necessary for the activity at hand. We do this all the time, though generally with little awareness in the matter. To be more intentional about it, we might identify specific characters that we can portray. To overcome a fear of public speaking, for example, we may draw upon the free-spirited extrovert inside us. The more we become aware of various personas that we put on, the more we learn to separate them from who we are deep down inside. This frees us up to bring out new aspects of ourselves or who we wish to become. Liberated from a rigid attachment to the identities we've held in the past, we free ourselves for personal transformation. This can be particularly powerful for those who seek redemption in one form or another.

Our inherent capacity for imagination is meant to enhance our lives, not to remove us or shelter us from life. It doesn't matter whether we imagine things that are positive or negative, optimistic or pessimistic, desired or unwanted. By envisioning any possibility, our attention begins to act upon the pure potentiality available to us at present, directing our personal power toward the fulfillment of that possibility.

Exercise 8b: Moment Artistry

Try to imagine the mind-frame of an athlete engaged in breaking a world record, or an explorer committed to survival in a gravely dangerous situation. Each of these individuals can only tap his or her personal best by fully engaging the moment at hand.

In much the same manner, *Moment Artistry* allows us to be fully present, to cooperate with the energies and possibilities presently available to us with a great sense of engagement, thereby bringing out the best in our work, play, and various interactions.

To begin this exercise, re-read the section on "Living in a State of Presence" on page 151. As you read the stories in that section, look for evidence of the six "presence" techniques exhibited therein. The Active Reflection process can help you develop any one of them as described on page 38. There are several, more specific steps that can be taken to develop *Moment Artistry* while integrating the various other techniques into the process:

STEP 1: CENTERING

The purpose of this activity is to bring your awareness fully into your body, connecting you with your physicality, sensuality, sexuality, emotion, brilliance, and spirituality in a balanced manner. By awakening the totality of your being, you enable yourself to more fully inhabit the present moment. To begin, seat yourself in a comfortable position. Take a deep breath, and let it slowly out. Allow yourself to become aware of the life-force inside you. Try to notice the beating of your heart and the blood flowing through your veins. Think about the energies in flow throughout your cells and tissues. Draw your attention to the center-point of your body—just below the navel in the core of your abdomen. Imagine this region as a kind of power cell that fuels your entire being. Feel this core energy radiating up into your heart to support the vitality of your physical body. Feel it radiating down through your crotch and legs, grounding and invigorating you. Feel it nourishing your skin and senses, activating your awareness of the things around you. Feel it lighting up your intelligence, filling it with an abundant brilliance. Now imagine roots growing down from this center-point into the earth, further grounding you. Imagine yourself as solid and magnificent as a giant redwood tree. Feel yourself expanding to an extraordinary capacity. Do this for five minutes or more, and you may experience a quieting of mind. It may seem like the world is slowing down. It may feel like you are suddenly tapping into a well of power deep within your being, or even beyond. Once you center yourself in this manner, observe how your experience of present circumstances is altered.

STEP 2: COMMUNION

We often see ourselves as the main characters in our lives, promoting a self-centered approach to everything we do. Communion enables us to enter the scene from a more expanded viewpoint, recognizing the various beings and forces at play all around us. Just as *centering* connects us with our holistic sense of being, *communion* deepens our awareness of the interconnections that we share with the whole of the world. To begin this activity, seat yourself in a comfortable position and engage in the centering exercise above. Once centered, recognize your location in the environment around you. Recognize someone or something nearby, and try to imagine your environment from that point of view. *What might be different about that perspective? How might it be similar to your own?* As you expand your awareness in this manner, notice any resonance you feel with the things around you. *Where or how do they resonate with you?* Do not try to do anything or change anything. Simply allow yourself to commune with the world around you. Try to feel it with your eyes closed. Drink it in. Taste it. Hear it. Smell it. See it in your mind's eye. Imagine it pervading every aspect of your being, temporarily blurring the perceived boundary between you and everything else.

STEP 3: PROCESS

Two sailors course along the surface of the ocean in a small craft. They have no control over the wind, or the waves, or the current, or the changing sky. Their art comes in interacting with these things, collaborating with them while taking their journey. *Process* is the art of sailing the greater flow of energies within and around you, working with them rather than against them. Though you may have set out on a desired course, you hold a majority of your attention to the conditions at play—the actual forces with which you may collaborate. *Process orientation* is the art of making the most of each moment along a greater path. Whether you are sailing, writing a paper, playing a game, attending the garden, or building a business, your effectiveness is guided by what you give of yourself to each moment, each step of the way. Sometimes you find yourself driven off course; other times, you find yourself in a zone of nearly effortless action, headed exactly where you wish to be going. Remember that success is not accomplished in a straight line motion, but by making the most of unexpected twists and turns that arise along the way. Trust in the process, and progress is guaranteed.

STEP 4: RADIANCE

Have you ever gazed into someone's eyes and felt as if you could see the essence of their consciousness in their very gaze? Maybe it seemed like a shallow veil, glistening across the surface of their eyes. Maybe it was deeper, like a quiet pond inside, rippling in gentle response to your interactions. Maybe it was vast as an ocean—awesome, yet mysterious. The more present we are at any given moment, the more transparently our innermost sense of self emanates from within, coalescing with the people and things around us. A half hour of free time each day can serve as a doorway to this state of being. You mustn't simply spend this time engaging in routine activities or hobbies, however. Begin by centering yourself without any preconceptions of how the time will be spent. Gaze around at your surroundings as if you've never seen them before. Do not ask yourself what you should do; rather, wait until you feel called forth into something unusual. The best thing that could possibly happen is that you spend your first few sessions in absolute boredom. Intentional boredom is like a void from which inspiration can emerge that is germane to the unique circumstances at hand. This inspiration is likely to catalyze the radiant emanation of your innermost self. Give it your best. Then see what happens.

STEP 5: CEREMONY

What if any given task is not simply something we have to do or accomplish, but rather, an opportunity to reveal ourselves? By honoring even the most mundane tasks with a reverence, as if they are somehow sacred, we can unearth the magic bound within each moment. Our inherent best is then freed to artfully emerge through empowered actions in a fulfilling manner. To use this technique, simply approach any situation you are in as if it is a ceremony, a rite, or a choice place to be. Use it as an opportunity to recognize and appreciate the gifts inherent in yourself and your life. Honor these gifts with the attitude of one who is experiencing a sacred moment. Draw upon them to offer this single moment the quality it deserves. This kind of ceremony is not about engaging in repetitive rituals, but rather, honoring the magic of the moment with the heart of a romantic, the thoughtfulness of a genius, the courage of a warrior, and the care of a humble, yet masterful student.

Most of us from young-adulthood on feel a need for more time in our lives. Consider the strange possibility, however, that what we actually need is less of it. By detaching ourselves from our mental adherence to the endless string of moments that we are used to living in—*time*—we open ourselves to a world of possibilities that beckon our attention to the expansiveness of each present moment. We soon bring the best in ourselves to whatever it is we are doing.

One of the most powerful means of oppressing someone, or even an entire population of people, is to convince them that they have little-to-no free time. Take a minute to consider the extent to which you yourself may hold the belief *that you have limited free time.* If this belief is at play, consider how it may affect your daily experience of life. *Do you ever feel like a slave to the many things you must do each day?* The purpose of this consideration is not to relieve you of your various commitments or obligations, but rather, to help you recognize that your sense of responsibility to an endless stream of tasks can actually diminish your effectiveness and enthusiasm in fulfilling any given one of them.

Moment artistry is a way of marrying *action* with *an interior experience of being* in that action. It is a means of courting your own vitality, and of being awake and alive through each passing moment—no matter how challenging, painful or invigorating that moment may feel.

AFTERWORD:
BEING VERSUS DOING

Every block of stone has a statue inside it,
and it is the task of the sculptor to discover it.

—MICHELANGELO, artist, architect and engineer (1475–1564)

When I was five years old, my uncle sat me down one Sunday morning and said, "Tell me Scotty, what do you want to be when you grow up?"

I stared at him, feeling rather confused by the question. Wasn't I already the person I was supposed to be?

"It's important that you start thinking about this," he explained. His kind eyes filled me with a sense of encouragement.

"I want to be like you," I said.

He smiled. "Finance can be a very lucrative field. Do you know what five plus five is?"

He seemed to be speaking a foreign language, but I was pretty sure that I knew the answer to his question. "Ten?" I asked.

"Good boy," he said. He winked at me.

As the years passed, a growing number of adults seemed to find interest in asking the same strange question over and over again. *What do you want to be when you grow up?*

"I want to be a fireman," I proclaimed one afternoon. I was promptly patted on the head, which somehow led me to believe that "fireman" was the wrong answer. I explored various answers such as "race car driver," "astronaut," "rock star," "president" and "teacher." Each was similarly dismissed, often with a charmed smile or a pat on the head.

One Thanksgiving dinner, my grandmother commented, "you're very good with science, Scotty. You should be a doctor." The adults in the room suddenly sat up in their seats, gazing at me with a kind of wishful eagerness.

A little more than a decade later, I graduated from college with a degree in mammalian physiology and set out on the lucrative path of a medical researcher. I landed a position in the field of disease studies, which excited my family to no end. Strangely, at the end of each workday I found myself standing in the shower under a cold stream of water trying to cleanse myself of the hours spent in the lab.

My pursuit of medicine had been an *intellectual* endeavor. It had been driven by *ideas* about what I ought *to do* with my life. Walking down that path, I had lost touch with the heart and spirit of what made me feel most alive, and with the elemental sense of *being* that might otherwise have directed my every step. As a result, I was not contributing the best of myself to the people and world around me.

It was around this time that I was introduced to Michelangelo's belief that the role of a sculptor was to discover the form inherent in the stone, and to simply chip away all the extraneous pieces until the form itself was revealed.

What if I began to apply a similar approach to sculpting my own life? What form might I find deep within me?

Scientific training had taught me to observe various natural phenomena in the world and develop insights based on those observations. It occurred to me that I might use this very discipline—much like Michelangelo's hammer and chisel—to chip away at the extraneous parts of myself in order to gain greater clarity about my innermost sense of being, if such a thing existed. I began to raise big questions, wielding them like the sculptor's chisel.

What if my path in life was not about the work that I chose to do, so much as it was about the parts of me that showed up to do that work? What if I allowed a sense of being to give rise to the doings that filled my time, rather than the other way around? What great spirit inside might then begin to reveal itself?

Looking back with some degree of scientific objectivity over the history of my deepest interests and most enjoyed activities, I noticed that from an early age I had been fascinated by the nature of human development and social structures. I had felt called to the field of education for years now, but I had invested so much time and energy into being *a scientist* that it was hard to consider wiping the slate clean and starting over. Perhaps there was some extraneous matter here that I might chip away from my life in order to discover a deeper sense of purpose.

I decided to take a day off from work. I went to the park and sat in the grass to ponder the possibilities available to me. Interestingly, I noticed that a vast majority of the people in the park were either women of color, or the young, Caucasian children to whom they attended. I was struck by how happy the women and children seemed. Prior to this morning, I had arrogantly viewed nannies and housekeepers as lower-class servants, somehow less important than myself. At this very moment, however, while fathers and mothers were off at their jobs—many of them no doubt feeling miserable as I did in our so-called high-class, well paying professions— these nannies were giving the best of themselves to human beings who truly appreciated their gifts. Whether or not these women felt any sense of burden in their work, or in their lives, there was no evidence of it in their actions or expressions.

I thought about the numerous things that I myself felt burdened to do each day. What if I began to approach my various activities as opportunities for self-discovery, rather than as burdens or chores? What if every single act could serve to unfold a part of my being, and my level of commitment to each act determined whether that unfolding was for better or worse?

Walking home from the park that morning, I set the intention to bring the best of myself to everything I did for one week—however boring or mundane—as a means of discovering the best in myself. As the days passed, I brought greater quality to my work; I was more efficient; I was more satisfied; I felt more alive. I gained new insights on who I was becoming and where I was going. I positioned myself for greater success in many aspects of my life. Within one week, I found myself gravitating toward those activities that filled me with the greatest sense of purpose.

After a month, I left the field of medical research and started a tutoring business. I experienced many failures in my first year of operation. Fortunately, my scientific training had taught me that *failure* was not something to be avoided. In science, you sometimes learn more from your failed experiments than you do from your successes. By embracing each failure and mining it for wisdom, I chipped away at those extraneous bits of minutia in my life to reveal the deeper sense of being that drove my various doings. I felt as if I was awakening from a deep slumber, opening my eyes to the true majesty that the world had to offer.

To approach each act in life with a spirit of excellence and experimentation—giving the best of yourself to everything you do—you open a doorway to that one-of-a-kind human being deep within. You reveal the brilliance and power of your unique inner form to yourself, and to everyone around you. No matter how badly you fail at times, you drive yourself to carry on. You chip away the extraneous matter that complicates your life, and develop the ability to approach everything you do from a simple, core sense of being.

As you work to develop the arts explored in this book, recognize that your unique sense of being unfolds with greater power and purpose when you give it the best you have to offer—even if ten minutes a day is all the time you that you choose to invest in this process.

Usersguidetobeinghuman.com offers advanced coursework and various forms of support to aid and encourage you along the way, as does the appendix to follow.

In closing, I'd like to share the words of Mahatma Gandhi who once declared: "You must be the change you want to see in the world."

Why not be that change today?

Go Shining!

SCOTT EDMUND MILLER

Appendix:
Tutorial for Forming a
"Reflection Group"

Reading without reflecting is like eating without digesting.

—EDMUND BURKE, statesman, political theorist and philosopher (1729–1797)

As Chapter 2 described, reflection is a powerful means of developing understanding. When this process is shared with colleagues, friends, or family members, the experience is even more powerful, as there are multiple minds available for processing experiences and information. They catalyze one another into a heightened, collective brilliance—as if joining to form a single, greater mind. The social experience is therefore an essential component of learning and growth. This is one of the reasons that book groups have endured as long as there have been books.

A "Reflection Group" allows participants to tap into a shared wealth of life experience and wisdom. Members must convene at least once every two weeks or so for the process to effectively unfold. Grounding this meeting with a set time and regular activities will enhance the experience. If time allows, it is best to begin each meeting with a shared meal or activity. Avoid mood-altering substances, as the purpose of this group is to bring out your inner capacities consciously and powerfully.

To form a reflection group that inspires and promotes your growth by using this book or any other material, begin by rereading the section on "Nourishing Your Intelligence" on page 27. Then take the following steps:

Step 1: Establish Membership

Identify people who potentially share your interest in personal growth. Make a list, including colleagues, friends and family members. Consider peers, as well as people younger and older than yourself. Diversity is a powerful promoter of growth, as it incorporates multiple perspectives and life experiences into the reflection process. Organize your list into three categories: (a) the person or people you believe will inspire and bring out the best in you through shared reflection, (b) those who might not inspire, but could nonetheless share the benefits of this process with you, and (c) those people who are likely to inhibit or resist the process, reducing your potential for growth. Cross out the people who fit in the third category, even if they are your closest companions.

STEP 2: IDENTIFY YOUR PURPOSE

Identify your purpose for expansion and growth by writing it down in a simple statement. Consider the following example, and modify it to meet your own personality and goals: "I am intent on developing the capacities with which I was born in a challenging and supportive reflection group; together, my partners and I will explore the art and science of self, inspiring one another to awaken our personal best."

STEP 3: INVITE MEMBERS TO A MEETING

Meet with the person or people on your "a" list. Share with them your statement of purpose, and invite them to form a reflection group with you. If you feel that you'd benefit from a larger circle, continue this process with some or all of the people on your "b" list. If you like, invite your partners to develop their "a" lists as well to bring more members to the group. You may wish to discuss these potential new members in order to ensure that you are in agreement on appropriate choices for participants.

STEP 4: SCHEDULE MEETINGS

Choose a recurring time weekly or bimonthly to meet with this team. If some people can only commit to one meeting a month, recognize that they are currently unable to make the commitment necessary for this work to be effective.

STEP 5: FORM AGREEMENTS

Form agreements with your group-mates about how you will interact with one another in order to best support each others' growth in an environment that provides intellectual and emotional safety. For example: *We agree to assume the best of each others' comments, suggestions, and actions. We agree to refrain from antagonistic criticism. We agree to take intellectual risks, and support one another in doing so. We agree not to repeat anything that is shared in our discussions outside our meetings. We agree to be on time, unless there are extenuating circumstances. We agree to read the assigned material prior to each meeting, and engage in the assigned exercises. We agree to have fun!*

STEP 6: SELECT LEADERSHIP

Someone should take the lead to organize and run each meeting. This need not be the same person each time. He or she should create a basic agenda to follow during the meeting that will help to establish an efficient use of your time together. The agenda can be modified as time goes on, adapted to support your ever-evolving work together (see the sample agenda to follow). If you encourage different members to lead each meeting, help provide them with tools for managing the meeting efficiently and effectively such as support in sticking to the agenda, managing time, asking questions that stimulate discussion, reading the material at least two times prior to the meeting to be very familiar with the concepts, to organize activities and discussion questions, and so on. Assign a separate timekeeper to help the session leader and the group stay on track.

The following agenda offers an example of how to structure meetings in a manner that maximizes the group's reflection time together.

Weekly *User's Guide* Reflection Group (Sample Agenda)

Meeting Facilitator: _____

Meeting Timekeeper:_____

6:00 p.m. Potluck Meal Break bread together and take time to connect. This is the place for catching up with each other and if you like, engaging in small-talk.

7:00 p.m. Centering Be absolutely prompt, honoring the time that you have set aside for your studies together. If some members are not yet present, begin without them. Gather in a circle and set a group intention to be present, focused and nonjudgmental of one another. This is a good time to review the group agreements.

7:05 p.m. Touching-In Allow each member to reflect on the week past, and share personal experiences regarding exercises assigned by the group during the last gathering. Remind people to be focused in what they share so that all participants have time to participate. Catching up and small-talk should have taken place during the potluck meal.

7:45 p.m. Discussion Analyze this week's assigned reading together, seeking to help one another deeply understand the material. Share personal insights or stories that deepen a collective understanding of the material. Again, remind participants to be focused in their comments.

8:30 p.m. Assignment Set an assigned reading and/or exercise for the coming week, drawing from exercises that correspond with the chapter material. *Note: assigned readings should be completed prior to the "reflection group" meeting.*

8:50 p.m. Meeting Evaluation Discuss how the meeting went, and suggest improvements for future meetings. If necessary, add to your list of group agreements. It is very important to be encouraging of this particular session's leader by offering specific comments about things that he or she did that provided value to the group. Leadership is a challenging activity, and should be honored. If discussions strayed from the topic, those responsible should own their actions and set the intention to be more focused in the next meeting.

9:00 p.m. Closing Be absolutely prompt, respecting the personal lives and obligations of group members. Assign a couple members each week to help with cleanup.

More information and support materials are available at: usersguidetobeinghuman.com (See page 184 for details.)

INDEX

Age of the
Human Capacities Revolution

It is my mission to empower people in all walks of life by helping them understand and awaken the extraordinary capacities that are freely available within them. How might society be improved if our millions upon millions of everyday citizens begin to tap their true potential? How might your life be affected if neighbors, coworkers, friends, family, and fellow community members learned to think clearly, communicate effectively, listen attentively, solve problems creatively, behave compassionately, and give the best of themselves to everyone around?

My colleagues and I are working to integrate *The User's Guide* and other important human capacities material into public school systems, social services, rehabilitation programs, mature-adult support organizations, and so on. If you would like to support our efforts by partnering with our organization, or by volunteering or donating to our cause, please visit usersguidetobeinghuman.com for more information. Be a part of the next great societal movement: *the Human Capacities Revolution*. Your involvement will make an important impact on the future of humanity.

ABOUT THE AUTHOR

As a human development theorist, educator, and school developer, Scott Miller has been involved in educational reform for more than a decade. He was the cofounder of Our Community School (OCS), a public charter school in Los Angeles, and served as the board chairman and CEO when OCS was recognized as the 2009 "Charter School of the Year" in the State of California. He recently cofounded a center to integrate educational programs based on *The User's Guide to Being Human* into public school systems and community services.

Mr. Miller's mission is to empower people of all ages and in all walks of life to harness the great potential that is freely available within them. *The User's Guide to Being Human* describes his theories and methods of self-development to make this possible. Synthesizing 5000 years of global wisdom on the topic of human capacities development, his work puts everyday men, women, and children in touch with the innate arts and sciences that drive the unfolding of their lives.

Scott is an avid hiker, and wrote much of this book while frequenting various trails in the quiet desert regions of Southern California. At the time of publishing this work, he is daydreaming at a fair clip along various California trails to develop his second book.

To learn more, visit his website at:
usersguidetobeinghuman.com

User's Guide Support Materials

Please visit usersguidetobeinghuman.com to learn about the *User's Guide* Workbooks:

- Eight individual workbooks are available that correspond with the eight chapters in this book. Each workbook is roughly 70 to 100 pages.
- Each workbook provides a personal tracking journal and various self-assessment tools.
- Each workbook offers worksheets and detailed support for the corresponding chapter exercises.
- Each workbook offers additional exercises not contained in this book.
- Each workbook includes a checklist that organizes your personal development work.
- Each workbook provides a detailed tutorial and worksheet on how to form a "Reflection Group."
- Each "Reflection Group" tutorial offers a detailed, eight-week curriculum on how to use the workbook and how to run your meetings.

The *User's Guide* workbooks can be downloaded directly from the site. Other resources are available on the site as well to support your efforts in effectively developing the eight arts explored in this book.